I0110211

God, Guns, Capitalism, and Hypermasculinity

EQUITY
IN HIGHER EDUCATION
THEORY, POLICY, & PRAXIS

Virginia Stead, H.B.A., B.Ed., M.Ed., Ed.D.
GENERAL EDITOR

VOL. 16

The Equity in Higher Education Theory, Policy, & Praxis series
is part of the Peter Lang Education list.
Every volume is peer reviewed and meets
the highest quality standards for content and production.

PETER LANG
New York • Bern • Berlin
Brussels • Vienna • Oxford • Warsaw

Warren J. Blumenfeld

God, Guns, Capitalism, and Hypermasculinity

Commentaries on the Culture of Firearms in the United States

PETER LANG
New York • Bern • Berlin
Brussels • Vienna • Oxford • Warsaw

Library of Congress Cataloging-in-Publication Data

A catalog record for this book has been requested

Bibliographic information published by **Die Deutsche Nationalbibliothek**.
Die Deutsche Nationalbibliothek lists this publication in the "Deutsche
Nationalbibliografie"; detailed bibliographic data are available
on the Internet at http://dnb.d-nb.de/.

ISSN 2330-4502 (print)
ISSN 2330-4510 (online)
ISBN 978-1-4331-9186-2 (paperback)
ISBN 978-1-4331-9187-9 (ebook pdf)
ISBN 978-1-4331-9188-6 (epub)
DOI 10.3726/b18831

© 2021 Peter Lang Publishing, Inc., New York
80 Broad Street, 5th floor, New York, NY 10004
www.peterlang.com

All rights reserved.
Reprint or reproduction, even partially, in all forms such as microfilm,
xerography, microfiche, microcard, and offset strictly prohibited.

This book is dedicated to all the victims of gun violence, their loved ones, and to the courageous and moral firearms safety activists who promote firearms safety legislation while countering a longstanding and seemingly entrenched culture of firearms in the United States.

Contents

Introduction & Overview

The Gun Culture Is Encoded into the DNA of U.S. Identity

We pledge allegiance to gun manufacturers and the NRA of America, and for campaign funds for which they give, we sacrifice, under God, our integrity and compassion for all.

The Pledge Taken by Too Many Politicians

The framers of the United States guaranteed its "free" people a right to carry and shoot terrifying weapons, but enslaved countless people transported against their will from the African continent to serve as dehumanized beasts of burden.

The framers of the United States guaranteed its "free" people a right to carry and shoot terrifying weapons but give the right of voting only to those who showed their white and male credentials.

The framers of the United States guaranteed its "free" people a right to carry and shoot terrifying weapons but robbed the people who had preceded them by thousands of years of their lands, cultures, livelihoods, and very lives.

The framers of the United States guaranteed its "free" people a right to carry and shoot terrifying weapons but considered no provisions for the universal education of its people.

The framers of the United States guaranteed its "free" people a right to carry and shoot terrifying weapons but disallowed girls and women to attend most institutions of higher education or to hold property on their own.

The framers of the United States guaranteed its "free" people a right to carry and shoot terrifying weapons but made no provisions in the implementation of quality affordable healthcare as a universal right and condition of a civil society.

The framers of the United States guaranteed its "free" people a right to carry and shoot terrifying weapons but abandoned its people to fend for themselves in their retirement years and in times of economic and physical hardships with few or no safety nets of security.

The framers of the United States guaranteed its "free" people a right to carry and shoot terrifying weapons but neglected to provide a regulatory mechanism to better sustain our natural resources and protect the planetary environment.

While wise men most who crafted what many consider today as a brilliant and enduring blueprint for a new nation, they were products of their times with their individual human shortcomings and biases. Just coming off a war of independence against one of the world's great colonial powers, leaders thought it reasonable to ensure the "free" people the capability of defending themselves against any potentially tyrannical government. In this regard, they established the Second Amendment in its Bill of Rights granting people "the right to bear arms."

Since then, firearms and the culture supporting it has been encoded into the very DNA of U.S.-American identity and what it means to be "an American." But what may have been "reasonable" in the 18th century, without substantial reform stands as unreasonable today.

A Brief History

The Chinese around 850 of the Common Era invented a powdery mixture of sulfur, charcoal, and potassium nitrate that when ignited with a spark, created an explosion. Though they discovered it quite accidently when attempting to invent an elixir for immortality, they quickly utilized it for defensive and offensive advantages in wars against internal and cross-border enemies (Kelly, 2004).

First used to stuff tubes in which the Chinese tied a fuse and lighted to propel as a hand-held rocket aimed at their adversaries, gun power transformed the "art" and scale of killing the likes of which the world had never seen. Throughout the decades and centuries in countries across the planet, the technology created even more and deadlier types of "hand cannons" as they were once called.

Attributed to the Portuguese in the 1400s, the "matchlock mechanism" was added to become the first known mechanically-firing gun. They attached a wick to a clamp that when triggered, sprang into the gun power. The Spanish carried these with them on their invasions into the Americas, and the Pilgrims brought them from England when they arrived in what would become known as North America (Saidel, 2000).

Christopher Columbus took with him matchlocks and other types of hand cannons and breech-loading wrought-iron weapons and arquebuses – an early type of portable firearm supported on a tripod or a forked rest. When he sailed from Haiti, he ordered shots fired through the shipwrecked hull of the Santa Maria to frighten indigenous populations with the power of European firearms (Saidel, 2000).

European inventors in 1509 replaced wicks with friction-wheel mechanisms to create the wheellock guns. These generated sparks to ignite the gun power. Later, as would become common in Colonial America, residents used flintlock guns invented around 1630 with flint-ignition mechanisms.

The Long Rifle ("Kentucky Rifle," "Pennsylvania Rifle") developed with spiral grooves giving iron balls a spiraling motion, which improved overall stability and accuracy. Combatants used these firearms as major weaponry during the so-called French and Indian War as well as in the American Revolutionary War.

At the end of the 16th century in Germany and other European countries, firearms technicians came up with a "wheel gun" (revolver) that included a revolving cylinder containing several chambers and at least one barrel for firing. Now shooters no longer had to reload following each shot but could unload up to six bullets at their intended targets. In the U.S., Samuel Colt in 1836 mass produced these multi-shot guns, popularly called "six shooters" (Chase, 2003).

By the 1850s, shot guns (also referred to as scatterguns) became popular. Usually fired from the shoulder, they use a single-fixed shell to fire numerous small spherical pellets called "shot" or a solid projectile called a "slug." Today, these firearms range from single action to semi- and fully automatic.

The Union forces in 1862 popularized the Gatling gun, developed by Richard Gatling, as a weapon of mass destruction. This rapid-fire gun was the forerunner of the machine gun. And then, the Cartridge Revolver, developed by Colt in 1872, was a .44-caliber rear loading weapon (Taffin, 2016). And the technology with its capacity to injure, mutilate, dismember, and kill increases with each passing day.

If Leif Erikson, the first known European to set foot on North America had been fully familiar and comfortable with gun powder and its destructive properties, there is little doubt that he would have brought firearms to those shores.

Comparing and Contrasting

Before and up to 1996, Australia had relatively high rates of murder, but a tragic incident at Port Arthur, Tasmania, April 28, 1996, was the proverbial straw that broke the poor camel's back. On that date, a man opened fire on a group of tourists killing 35 and wounding another 23. The massacre was the worst mass murder in Australia's history (Brigham, 1996).

Taking decisive action, newly-elected *conservative* Prime Minister, John Howard, negotiated a bipartisan deal between the national, state, and local governments in enacting comprehensive gun safety measures, which included a massive buyback of more than 600,000 semi-automatic rifles and shotguns, and laws prohibiting private firearms sales, mandatory registration by owners of all weapons, and the requirement that all potential buyers of guns at the time of purchase give a "genuine reason" other than general or overarching self-defense without documentation of necessity.

By 1996, polls showed overwhelming public support of approximately 90% for the new measures. And though firearms-related injuries and deaths have not totally come to an end, homicides by firearms fell by 59% between 1995 and 2006 with *no* corresponding increase in non-firearm-related homicides, and a 65% reduction in gun-related suicides (Oremus, 2017).

In addition, there has been significant drops in robberies involving firearms, and contrary to fears by some, no increase in the overall number of home invasions. In the decade preceding the Port Arthur massacre, Australia recorded 11 mass shootings. No mass shootings have occurred in the 20+ years since the measures went into effect as of 2016 (Fox, 2016).

Just six day after the recent terrible hate-inspired gun murders of Muslims praying at two Mosques in Christchurch New Zealand, Prime Minister Jacinda Ardern announced sweeping new firearms regulations, which included banning semi-automatic rifles and large-capacity ammunition magazines, and a mandatory government buyback of such previously sold weapons.

The events perpetrated by a deadly shooter at Marjorie Stoneman Douglas High School on February 14, 2018 in Parkland, Florida may have signaled that watershed enough-is-enough moment as courageous student leaders and the movement they spawned seemed to have tipped the balance of power on the issue of the place of firearms in the United States. This alongside the withdrawal of key contributors and commercial enterprises and financial drains resulting from state lawsuits, by 2019, the National Rifle Association was reaching economic crisis. In addition, upheaval within its leadership structure placed the NRA is a severely weakened position in terms of its overall ability and effectiveness in its lobbying efforts and capacity to attract substantially increasing new membership.

This book includes a selection of my editorial commentaries focusing on this critical debate on the place of firearms in U.S. society and culture.

References

Bingham, M. (1996). *Suddenly one Sunday*. Sydney, Australia: Harper Collins.

Chase, K. (2003). *Firearms: A global history to 1700*. Cambridge, UK: Cambridge University Press.

Fox, M. (2016, June 22). No mass shootings in Australia in 20 years: How did they do it? NBC News Online.

Kelly, J. (2004). *Gunpowder: Alchemy, bombards & pyrotechnics: The history of the explosive that changed the world*. New York: Basic Books.

Oremus, W. (2017, October 2). In 1996, Australia enacted strict gun laws. It hasn't had a mass shooting since. *Slate*, n.p.

Saidel, B. (2000). Matchlocks, Flintlocks, and Saltpetre: The chronological implications for the use of Matchlock muskets among Ottoman-period Bedouin in the Southern Levant. *International Journal of Historical Archaeology, 4*(3), 191–216.

Taffin, J. (12 August 2016). Colt's finest single action. In J. Lee (ed.). *Gun Digest 2017*. (71 ed.). pp. 96–106.

Section One

Capitalism/Government

Chapter One

A Civics Lesson on the Second Amendment

A well-regulated militia being necessary to the security of a free State, the right of the People to keep and bear arms shall not be infringed.
Second Amendment, United States Constitution

As we learned in junior high school civics class, laws undergo various processes to become enacted and enforced. Through our system of federalism, legislative bodies on the national, state, and local levels write and pass laws, which are then signed and enforced by the executive branches and judged as falling within or out of constitutional guidelines by the justices in the judicial branches.

Throughout the process in the development of the Constitution and ever since, people have engaged in often heated debates over what even the smallest word and concept should and does mean. Though the framers of the Constitution imposed "the right of the People to keep and bear arms," as with all laws, our legislators and, more specifically, our judiciary defines its parameters.

To engage in a reasoned discussion from the same vantage point, we must study not only the precise or strict text of a law or regulation, but also investigate the supporting or modifying laws and rulings related to it. For example, the U.S. Supreme Court has expanded (clarified) the definition of "A well-regulated militia." The Court, in its 2008 ruling in *District of Columbia v. Heller* extended the right to individuals. From the ruling:

"The Second Amendment guarantees an individual right to possess a firearm unconnected with service in a militia, and to use that arm for traditionally lawful purposes, such as self-defense within the home." That right, however, "is not unlimited."

Though the types of firearms at the writing of the Constitution appear rather primitive compared with the technologically evolved weapons of today, in 2016, the Court ruled on this point in *Caetano v. Massachusetts*:

> The Court has held that the Second Amendment extends, *prima facie*, to all instruments that constitute bearable arms, even those that were not in existence at the time of the founding, and that this Second Amendment right is fully applicable to the States.

So, does this mean that all firearms, even the military-style semiautomatic or so-called "assault" weapons, must be available for sale to individuals under constitutional law?

In four separate cases in different federal Circuit Courts of Appeals, judges ruled that states placing bans on semi-automatic weapons, are, in fact, constitutional, and that the *Heller* decision excluded these types of weapons. Therefore, individual state laws were upheld.

1. Washington, DC, Circuit, 2011: Assault weapons and large capacity magazines are "too dangerous for self-defense reasons."
2. 7th Circuit, Chicago, 2015: Upheld a ban on "any semiautomatic gun that can accept a large-capacity magazine." Also, the concept of Federalism allows local municipalities to enact gun safety restrictions.
3. 2nd Circuit, New York & Connecticut, 2015: Unanimous ban: "semiautomatic assault weapons have been understood to pose unusual risks," resulting in "more numerous wounds, more serious wounds, and more victims. These weapons are disproportionately used in crime, and particularly in criminal mass

shootings like the attack in Newtown. They are also disproportionately used to kill law enforcement officers."

4. 4th Circuit, Richmond, 2017: Maryland's ban on 45 kinds of
assault weapons and its 10-round limit on gun magazines were
upheld as constitutional.

To date, the United States Supreme Court has decided not to review
these lower court rulings.

The U.S. Congress enacted a brief federal ban on assault weapons,
The Public Safety and Recreational Firearms Use Protection Act, in
September 1994. The ban, which also included barring high-capacity
magazines, expired in September 2004 as required in its 10-year sunset
provision. The measure has not since been reauthorized by Congress.
Many of the violent mass shooters since the ban expired used semi-
automatic rifles with large-capacity ammunition magazines, including
at Sandy Hook in 2012 and at Marjory Stoneman Douglas High School
in Parkland, Fla., in 2018.

As a provision inserted as a rider into the 1996 federal government omnibus spending bill, the Dickey Amendment, named
after Arkansas Republican Representative Jay Dickey and lobbied
heavily by the National Rifle Association, passed the Congress
into law. It mandated that "none of the funds made available for
injury prevention and control at the Centers for Disease Control and
Prevention (CDC) may be used to advocate or promote gun control"
(Jamaison, 2013).

How free, though, are any of us as an estimated 11,000+ people
are murdered annually, and another 22,000+ lose their lives by guns
through accident or suicide? How free are we as the guns lobby purchases our politicians in the service of firearms manufacturers in their
quest to acquire even more power and profits? By 2018 gun-related
deaths increased to 39,773 according to The Centers for Disease in
Atlanta, Georgia (Gstalter, 2018).

With the relatively easy access to firearms in the United States, few
of us have not already been touched by the ravages of gun violence.
Hardly a day goes by that we do not hear of yet another high visibil-
ity mass shooting, which does not even begin to reflect the seemingly

countless number of lives taken in small towns and large cities throughout the nation that don't make it to the national spotlight.

How many more of our precious people of all ages will have their lives cut short under the banner of "freedom to bear arms"?

What will it take for us to reverse the unholy alliance between corporate America and powerful pressure groups controlling politicians in the service of firearms manufacturers?

When is enough, enough?!

References

Gstalter, M. (2018, December 13). CDC report: US gun deaths reach highest level in nearly 40 years. *The Hill.* n.p.

Jamieson, C. (2013, February). *Gun violence research: History of the federal funding freeze. Psychological Science Agenda.* Washington, DC: American Psychological Association.

Chapter Two

God, Guns, & Capitalism

What appeared as a sick and extraordinarily insensitive stunt turned out to be an actual announcement (McChoppin, 2016) for a raffle to "benefit" the victims' families of the Orlando massacre at Pulse, an LGBTQ nightclub in which a shooter murdered 49 and wounded another 53 people in the early morning hours of June 12, 2016.

The owners of Second Amendment Sports of McHenry, Illinois sold tickets in their raffle for the prize of an AR-15 military-grade assault rifle, which is similar to the weapon of mass destruction and death used by the shooter at the Pulse nightclub. Raffle organizers eventually canceled the raffle not because of the outrage they received on the insensitivity of the event, but, rather, they realized that a raffle conducted by a for-profit company might be declared illegal in their state's judicial system.

Second Amendment Sports' heartless raffle represents only one installment in the volatile and explosive gun culture of the United States.

Spike's Tactical shop of Apopka, Florida marketed its special AR-15 assault rifle, which company spokesperson, Former Navy SEAL Ben "Mookie" Thomas, claimed (Curtis, 2015) was "designed to never be used by Muslim terrorists," as the shop's never-ending battle in the Christian Crusades.

On one side of the rifle, shop employees laser-etched the Knights Templar Long Cross of the original Crusaders when they marched to reclaim the Holy Land from Muslims in 1099 CE. On the other side, they engraved Psalm 144:1: "Blessed be the Lord my Rock, who trains my hands for war, my fingers for battle." Called "The Crusader," the rifle includes a three-setting trigger safety control branded "Peace," "War," and "God Wills It."

"Mookie" Thomas originated the idea for the rifle, stating, "Off the cuff I said I'd like to have a gun that if a Muslim terrorist picked it up, a bolt of lightning would hit and knock him dead."

Unfortunately, owners, employees, and customers at Spike's Tactical seemed to have forgotten that the Christian Crusades represent one of the most horrific, shameful, and tragic scars on Christendom. Pope Urban II summoned the First Crusade in Clermont, France to "liberate" Jerusalem from Muslims. In the summer of 1096, as the crusade began, they murdered several thousand Jews along their way in the lands along the Rhine River, looted and destroyed their homes, as the Crusaders stated, "Because why should we go off to attack the unbelievers in the Holy Land and leave the unbelievers in our midst untouched.?" They accused Jews as being treacherous auxiliaries of Muslims. According to Pope Urban II, "Let us first avenge ourselves on them [the Jews] and exterminate them from among the nations so that the name of Israel will no longer be remembered, or let them adopt our faith" (Beker, 2008).

When the Crusaders reached Jerusalem in 1099, they pillaged Muslim buildings and killed thousands. The massacre of the Muslim population of Jerusalem reached epic proportions. In addition, the invaders burned the synagogue on the Temple Mount to the ground with all the Jews inside. One Crusader, an eyewitness to the event wrote: "Men rode in blood up to their knees and bridal reins. It was a just and splendid judgment by God that this place would be filled with the blood of the unbelievers" (Peters, 1971).

The Crusades lasted from 1040 to 1350. By 1204, however, the tide began to turn against the Western European invaders, as the Mamluk dynasty in Egypt drove them out of Palestine and Syria.

In another installment in the booming and explosive gun culture, Bergeron's Restaurant in Louisiana, billing itself as the home of "God, Gumbo, and Guns," offers a 10% discount to any customer who brings a gun with them to lunch or dinner. Says restaurant owner Kevin Cox: "Show it to me out of your purse, out of your back pocket …. Show that you have one so if something goes wrong here today, I know you're here to protect me." Cox criticized gun-free businesses like Chipotle and Target: "You make a gun-free zone," he argued, "that's where bad people with guns are going to go – dumbest thing I've ever heard." In the first year since instituting the discount in 2014, business increased approximately 25% (CBS News, 2015).

Giving new meaning to the term "hunting for a wife," Jewelry by Harold owner in North Liberty, Iowa gave husbands-to-be a voucher for a new Remington 870 rifle with the purchase of an engagement ring priced at $1,999 or higher. Shop owner Harold van Beek stated: "So say: I'm hunting deer, and here is a diamond ring, dear" (Stusinski, 2012). To apply for this "deal," one must be eligible to own a gun in Iowa, and not have been convicted of a felony.

In its attempt to pull in shoppers on so-called "Black Friday" (the day following Thanksgiving), the camping and outdoors superstore, Cabela's, handed out envelopes to the first 800 people over the age of 18 who lined up in front of its stores before 5:00 a.m. for a chance to win a Browning A-Bolt Medallion .300 WSM rifle with a Cabela's 50th anniversary gun case worth $875.

And maybe it's not too late to go down to Nations Truck Sales in Sanford, Florida where they offered each customer a brand spanking new assault rifle with the purchase of a truck. Stated General Sales Manager, Nick Ginetta: "We started on Veterans Day. Hey, so many have given so much for this right!" (Kim, 2010).

I have heard about people being shot from canons, but for those who want to remain active hunters well after they have "bought the farm," now their wishes have come true. Be the first on your block to kill long after you have died. For the sum of only $1250, your loved ones can have you cremated with a pound of your ashes stuffed inside genuine bullets, resurrecting you as live ammunition. For that measly sum, you can metamorphose as 250 shot shells, 100 rifles cartridges, or

250 pistol cartridges. For only $100 extra, until you come alive again as a killing apparatus, your bullet ashes can rest in peace in a decorative wooden coffin-like box.

The company, Holy Smoke Bullet Urns of Stockton, Alabama, has taken quite literally Shylock's claim in Shakespeare's 1596 *Merchant of Venice*: "The pound of flesh which I demand of him is deerely bought, 'tis mine, and I will have it." According to the company's cofounder, Clem Parnell: "You know I've thought about this for some time and I want to be cremated. Then I want my ashes put into some turkey load shotgun shells and have someone that knows how to turkey hunt use the shotgun shells with my ashes to shoot a turkey. That way I will rest in peace knowing that the last thing that one turkey will see is me, screaming at him at about 900 feet per second" (Ingold, 2012).

Wow, in this way, you will obtain virtual immortality in the elk antlers hung over your family's fire place or in the stuffed duck sitting on their living room side table. In addition to the decimation of wild game, the company offers this alternative to traditional burial as a means to "continue to protect your home and family even after you are gone." So just think of it; now you can kill a home intruder by shooting them right in the gut with your Great Uncle Henry or Aunt Gert!

And just in time for the holiday season, the Scottsdale, Arizona gun club now offers its members the service of sending out their Christmas cards with family members, including infants, posing with Santa while holding pistols and military grade automatic weapons, fa la la la la, la la la la. Joy to the world? (*Daily Mail*, 2011).

I would ask, though, have so many in fact given so much for the right for us to turn our bodies literally into killing devices or for the right to own a "free" assault or hunting rifle? Do we really want "the last thing that one turkey will see is me, screaming at him at about 900 feet per second." Do residents of our nation really *need* so many guns, assault rifles and others?

The very first thing that caught my eye as I entered the grounds of the Iowa Republican Party Presidential Straw Poll in the summer of 2011 were three young children, I estimated between the ages of 4–7, wearing day-glow orange baseball caps with "NRA" [National

Rifle Association] scrawled atop, and round stickers on their T-shirts announcing "GUNS SAVE LIVES."

Of the mass murders in the United States since 1982, most of the shooters obtained their weapons *legally*. Demographically, the shooters in all but one case involved males usually white, with an average age of 35 years.

Certainly, Bergeron's, Jewelry by Harold, Cabela's, Holy Smoke Bullet Urns of Stockton, Alabama Nation's Truck Sales of Sanford, Florida, and gun clubs hold the constitutional right to market their devices of death, but what type of messages are they communicating? Are we really "free" as a society when our right "to keep and bear arms shall not be infringed"?

I propose that we reevaluate the political right's obsession with the so-called "freedom" to bear arms because it is *not* only "criminals who kill people" as Second Amendment advocates claim, and counter NRA Executive VP Wayne LaPierre argument that "The only thing that stops a bad guy with a gun is a good guy with a gun" (Memmott, 2012).

How many more Columbines and Auroras; Charleston's; Fort Hoods; Virginia Techs; Northern Illinois Universities; University of California's at Santa Barbara; Seattle Pacific Universities; Phoenix, Arizona parking lots; Pennsylvania Amish school houses; Santana High Schools; Springfield Oregon high schools; Jonesboro, Arkansas middle schools; Sandy Hooks and Stoneman Douglass High Schools, Universities of Texas; Honolulu, Hawaii Xerox Corporations; Atlanta brokerage offices; US postal offices; movie theaters, Jewish community centers and schools; Muslim community centers and Mosques; Sikh temples; Christian churches; outdoor music festivals; and U.S. highways? How many more dead to urban and suburban violence? How many more firearms-induced killings to domestic violence? How many more accidental killings of small children and adults?

And how many more Gabby Giffords, Harvey Milks, George Tillers, Tupac Shakurs, The Notorious B.I.Gs., Trayvon Martins, Lawrence Kings, Michael Browns, Tamir Rices, Alison Parkers, Adam Wades, Molly Judith Olgins, Mary Christine Chapas, Katherine Coopers, Richard Michaels-Martinezes, elementary school students and teachers, the famous, and the not-so-famous will it take for this country and its politicians to wake up to the reality that, contrary to the NRA's assertions, guns in the hands of *anyone*, in any and all stations of life, kill people?

References

Beker, A. (2008). *The chosen: The history of an idea, the anatomy of an obsession*. New York: Palgrave MacMillan. p. 106.

CBS News. (2015, January 2). Bergeron's restaurant: Home of God, gumbo and guns. https://www.cbsnews.com/news/gun-friendly-restaurant-in-louisiana-gives-carrying-customers-discount/.

Curtis, H. P. (2015, September 2). Assault rifle with Bible verse to repel Muslim terrorists unveiled in Apopka. *Orlando Sentinel*. n.p.

Daily Mail. (2011, November 28). I want an assault rifle for Christmas or the reindeer gets it! Gun club invites children to pose with Santa … and their choice of firearm. *Daily Mail*, n.p.

Ingold, S. (2012, November 13). At life's end, a final home on the (shooting) range. *NPR*, n.p.

Kim, S. (2010, November 19). Buy a truck, get a free AK-47 assault rifle. *ABC News*, n.p.

McChoppin, R. (2016, June 29). McHenry gun shop to raffle off AR-15 rifle to benefit Orlando shooting victims. *Chicago Tribune*, n.p.

Memmott, M. (2012, December 21). Only 'a good guy with a gun' can stop school shootings, NRA says. *NPR*, n.p.

Peters, E. (Ed.). (1971). The First Crusade: "The Chronicle of Fulcher of Chartres" and other source materials. Philadelphia: University of Pennsylvania Press. p. 260.

Stusinski, M. (2012, October 18). Buy A ring, get a free gun at Iowa jewelry store. *Inquisitr*. n.p.

Chapter Three

Government & Business Complicit

The term "pogrom" refers "to the deliberate persecution of an ethnic or religious group either approved or condoned by the local authorities" (Unionpedia). It has traditionally applied to the government supported or sponsored violence against Jews under the Russian Empire in the late 19th- through early 20th-centuries C.E. that spread throughout the Russian "Pale of Settlement," which included the area of governmental confinement of Jews in Eastern Europe.

Pogroms can include blatant and sustained acts of violence, for example, like that depicted at Tzeitel and Perchik's wedding reception in the Broadway musical *Fiddler on the Roof*, and murders and sacking of Jewish stores and homes during the infamous *Kristallnacht* ("Night of Broken Glass") between 9–10 November 1938 in Germany.

The gun violence in individual and mass murders and injuries throughout the U.S. falls under the category of pogroms. The country suffers an estimated 11,000 gun-related murders annually and another 22,000 accidental and suicidal deaths, reaching nearly 40,000 deaths by 2017 (Gstalter, 2018). While not necessarily government sponsored, these acts of domestic terrorism, these pogroms, are certainly government condoned.

Each politician who accepts money (bribes) from the firearms lobbyists, most notably from the National Rifle Association, conspires in the spate of pogroms plaguing the nation. In rare occasions, some state and local legislatures have passed modest laws in their attempts to reduce gun violence, and the U.S. Congress, with the backing of the NRA, passed meager background checks legislation. In the depths of these ever-increasing tragedies, however, the majority of legislators conspire with the gun lobbies who fire up their constituencies to a fever pitch to vote against any meaningful and comprehensive solutions to these pogroms.

Government-sponsored pogroms also include more subtle means to justify persecution of entire groups of people including the strategy of the propaganda of fear and agitation to sway public opinion. An historical example is the notorious *Protocols* (Minutes) *of a Meeting of the Learned Elders of Zion*. The *Protocols* was a fabricated antisemitic narrative dating from 1903 that was widely distributed by Russian Czarist forces to turn public opinion against a so-called "Jewish Marxist Revolution" for the purpose of convincing the populace that Jews were plotting to impose a conspiratorial international Jewish government. It is composed of the alleged minutes of a late 19th-century meeting where Jewish leaders planned to subvert the minds, morals, and cultures of non-Jews by controlling politicians, the press, and world economies for world domination. The *Protocols* was translated into many languages and circulated throughout the world.

In fact, the raging antisemite, Henry Ford, the U.S. automotive pioneer, argued that Jews controlled world leaders, international finance, and the media. He had the *Protocols* translated into English in 1927, and published in his newspaper, *The Dearborn* (Michigan) *Independent*, thereby introducing it to a large U.S. audience. Beginning in 1920, Ford chronicled what he considered the "Jewish menace" in his paper. Every week for the next 91 issues, Ford exposed some sort of Jewish evil. The most popular and virulent of his articles he chose to reprint into four volumes titled *The International Jew: The World's Foremost Problem*.

Adolph Hitler bestowed on Henry Ford the highest award given to a non-German, the Grand Cross of the German Eagle in 1938. Following WWII at the Nuremberg Trials, Baldur von Schirach, leader of Hitler Youth, stated that Hitler had become "Jew-wise" by reading Henry Ford's writings about the Jews.

Wayne LaPierre Jr., Executive VP of the National Rifle Association, as well as NRA spokesperson, Dana Loesch, spoke their brand of the propaganda of fear and agitation at the annual Conservative Political Action Conference (CPAC) in Maryland in 2018 when Loesch indicted the media: "Many in legacy media love mass shootings. You guys love it. Now I'm not saying that you love the tragedy. But I am saying that you love the ratings. Crying white mothers are ratings gold to you." (For those like myself who don't know what she means by "legacy media," I discovered a definition (Legacy Media) as "n. Primarily mature newspaper and television news outlets that believe they are the final word on any topic.")

Next, when it was LaPierre's turn to rant at CPAC, he brought out every tired clichéd buzzword in the ultra-conservatives' perennially-referenced playbook to attack and demean individuals and institutions holding anything other than the NRA's extremist positions on the Second Amendment (Abramson, 2018). Subsumed within his overarching nationalist theme of a "socialist enemy," which he claimed "oppose[s] our fundamental freedoms enshrined in the Bill of Rights," he embedded an anti-intellectual subtext by going after higher education.

Taking words that could have come directly from the mouth of Senator Joseph McCarthy (and the pages of the *Protocols*), LaPierre argued that the *Communist Manifesto* and all the works of Karl Marx were among the most assigned curricular materials, and he described socialism as "a political disease," to loud and boisterous cheers.

Warning the ballroom audience packed to overflowing: "You should be anxious, and you should be frightened. If these so-called European socialists take over the House and the Senate and, God forbid, they win the White House again, our American freedoms could be lost and our country will be changed forever, and the first to go will be the Second Amendment to the US constitution."

He accused "intellectual elites," who think they are "smarter and better," and oppose "free-market capitalism" and "restrict freedoms," in their "utopian dream" in pushing their "terrifying" and "freedom killing" style of "European-style Socialism."

To entice the minions in ways outside of fear and agitation, literally thousands of businesses throughout the country offer NRA members special exclusive discounts ranging from around 5% to as high as 40%. The scope of businesses run from car dealerships, building supplies, firearms sales, and restaurants, to legal services, banks, home and office surveillance systems, and "Anti-aging Solutions," and a seemingly unlimited more (NRA website, retrieved 9/8/2019).

Recently, however, as challenges to the power of the NRA have increased through the youth organized #MarchForOurLives movement, some private companies have decided to suspend sponsorship of these discounts. Such companies include First National Bank of Omaha, and Enterprise Holdings, with its car rental subsidiaries Enterprise, Alamo, and National (Shulte, 2018).

Gun violence plaguing the U.S. must not be dismissed as merely the actions of separated individual actors: the mentally ill, the disgruntled, the disposed, the marginalized, the ideological, the "bad guys." No, these actors play their roles in consort within a tightly-scripted narrative authored by the greedy, those scoring large profits and enormous degrees of power. Those of us who fail to stand up and interrupt the scene stand complicit in this fatal drama.

References

Abramson, A. (2018, February 22). NRA's Wayne LaPierre at CPAC: Gun control advocates are exploiting the Florida school shooting tragedy. *Time Magazine*, n.p.

Gstalter, M. (2018, December 13). CDC report: US gun deaths reach highest level in nearly 40 years. *The Hill*. n.p.

Legacy Media (retrieved 9/8/2019). https://www.urbandictionary.com/define.php?term=legacy%20media

NRA website (retrieved 9/8/2019). https://home.nra.org/.

Shulte, G. (2018, February 23). Bank, Enterprise parting with NRA following Florida school massacre. *Associated Press*, n.p. https://en.unionpedia.org/i/Pogrom.

Chapter Four

NRA CEO Warns of a Socialist Takeover of Guns

While I'm usually the last to use sports metaphors since I know so little about sports and care even less, I find it apt to assert that the new and dynamic youth-led gun safety movement, #MarchForOurLives, has pushed the National Rifle Association's leadership onto the ropes.

After each of the numerous high-profile mass gun tragedies over the past few decades or so, the NRA has typically maintained a relatively low profile and has remained virtually silent for a specific amount of time until headlines fade from view and the country's attention diverts elsewhere. Since the horrific massacre of 17 gentle souls, however, at Marjorie Stoneman Douglas High School in Parkland, Florida in 2018, the leadership of the NRA has spoken out by attacking everything and everyone from the so-called "legacy" and "fake" media, to community law enforcement and the "corrupt" FBI, to Hollywood, Washington, and even to the emerging student activists.

In fact, both Wayne LaPierre Jr., Executive VP of the National Rifle Association, as well as NRA spokesperson, Dana Loesch, co-opted one of #MarchForOurLives's phrases, "We Call BS," (Wyrich, 2018) used so effectively by one of its courageous leaders, Emma Gonzalez, a senior at Douglas High School. But to paraphrase an old truism, obvious and ineffectual attempts at cooptation are the highest forms of flattery!

LaPierre tossed out every tired clichéd buzzword in the ultra-conservatives' perennially-referenced playbook to attack and demean individuals and institutions holding anything other than the NRA's extremist positions on the Second Amendment. He accused "intellectual elites," who think they are "smarter and better," and oppose "free-market capitalism" and "restrict freedoms," in their "utopian dream" in pushing their "terrifying" and "freedom killing" style of "European-style Socialism." Any first-year psychology student will perceive the mechanism of projection in his claim that "socialism is a movement that loves to smear."

Subsumed within his overarching nationalist theme of a "socialist enemy," which he claimed "oppose[s] our fundamental freedoms enshrined in the Bill of Rights," he embedded an anti-intellectual subtext by going after higher education. Taking words that could have come directly from the mouth of Senator Joseph McCarthy, LaPierre warned that the *Communist Manifesto* and all the works of Karl Marx were among the most assigned curricular materials, and he described socialism as "a political disease," to loud and boisterous cheers.

Warning the ballroom audience packed to overflowing: "You should be anxious and you should be frightened. If these so-called European socialists take over the House and the Senate and, God forbid, they win the White House again, our American freedoms could be lost and our country will be changed forever, and the first to go will be the Second Amendment to the US constitution" (Smith, 2018).

LePierre tipped his hand that he not only fears the youth leading the fast-moving mobilization against gun violence, but also several strong voices in a new crop and old guard of political leaders that he singled out in his CPAC diatribe, some of whom were then potential 2020 presidential candidates. These were Senators Kamala Harris (D-CA), Elizabeth Warren (D-MA), Chris Murphy (D-CN), and Bernie Sanders (I-VT), and Representative Nancy Pelosi (D-CA).

Even before the Cold War and the so-called "McCarthy Era" (named after Wisconsin Senator, Joseph McCarthy), individuals and groups on the political and theocratic Right have flung the term "Socialist" as an expletive from their metaphoric sling shots into the faces of their political opponents to discredit their characters and dismiss their political ideas and policies, and to sway the electorate toward a conservative and nationalist agenda.

This continues to this very day as evidenced by opponents of Senator Bernie Sanders who has described himself as a "Democratic Socialist." Enemies of the Affordable Care Act often warned that its passage would march us down the devastating path of "European-style Socialism," oh my!

As destructive and as freedom-killing as the Right would have us believe, according to the World English Dictionary, Socialism involves "a theory or system of social organization that advocates the vesting of the ownership and control of the means of production and distribution, of capital, land, etc., in the community as a whole," where each of us has a stake and advances in the success of our collective economy (retrieved 9/8/2019).

No country in the world today stands as a fully Socialist state, but rather, some of the most successful economies combine elements of Capitalism with Socialism to create greater degrees of equity and lesser disparities between the rich, the poor, and those on the continuum in between.

Each year, the Organisation for Economic Co-operation and Development again conducted its annual "Better Life Index" (OECD, 2018) to determine the "happiest countries in the world," according to its residents. Based on an 11-measure survey assessing quality of life, including housing, income, jobs, community, education, the environment, health, work-life balance, and life satisfaction, all Scandinavian countries, plus Iceland, Netherlands, and Switzerland, and only one North American country, plus Australia, and New Zealand reached the top 10 ranked countries.

Included in descending order in the 2018 report are number one, Finland, followed by Norway, Denmark, Switzerland, Iceland, Netherlands, Canada (which provides a single-payer health care system unlike its North American neighbor, the United States), New Zealand, Sweden, and Australia (which places severe restrictions on firearms ownership and, thereby, has significantly reduced gun violence).

The United States did not make the cut in the top 10 falling to 15th. Therefore, we might do well to look to these countries for some of their "socialist" policies that sustain significantly higher levels of economic and social quality and vastly lower rates of gun-related and overall rates of violence and murders. (By 2020, the ranking had changed somewhat due to the effects of the Coronavirus, though all the Scandinavian countries remained within the top 10.)

But to LaPierre and other nationalist and "neoliberal" advocates of smaller government and massive deregulation of the private and corporate sectors, virtually any and every form of governmental regulation they label "socialistic." And though their battle cry of "liberty" and "freedom" through "individual personal responsibility" sounds wonderful on the surface, what are the costs of this alleged "liberty" and "freedom"?

How free and liberated are the estimated 11,000 people gunned down annually in the United States? And how free and liberated are their loved ones left behind? How free and liberated today are the viciously murdered 20 beautiful babies and six of their teachers and administrators at Sandy Hook Elementary School? How free and liberated are the 14 murdered teens and their three teachers at Marjorie Stoneham Douglas High School?

How truly free and liberated are we as a nation when a powerful lobbying group buys our politicians to vote for the special interests of the industrial firearms complex over the best interests of we the people and to the detriment of our democratic form of government?

LaPierre concluded his CPAC speech by repeating his delusional mantra that he introduced following the Sandy Hook school shooting in Newtown, Connecticut, in 2012: "To stop a bad guy with a gun, it takes a good guy with a gun."

No Wayne, to stop a bad guy with a gun, we as a society must craft and enact common sense regulations on the manufacture, sale, capacity, force, type, and number of firearms we are willing to allow so we may better ensure safer and more socially connected communities.

References

OECD. (2018). *Better life index.* Retrieved 9/8/2019, *http://www.oecdbetterlifeindex.org/top ics/life-satisfaction/*

Smith, D. (2018, February 22). NRA head breaks silence to attack gun control advocates: 'They hate individual freedom.' *The Guardian*, n.p.

Wyrich, A. (2018). The 6 wildest quotes from NRA spokeswoman Dana Loesch at CPAC, *Daily Dot*, 2/22/2018.

Chapter Five

NRA Pouring Blood Money on Politicians & Media

We need in every community a group of angelic troublemakers. *Our power is in our ability to make things unworkable.* The only weapon we *have* is *our* bodies, and we need to tuck them in places so wheels don't turn.

Bayard Rustin (Gadoua, 2015).

The "wheels" that Bayard Rustin, iconic civil rights leader and mentor, referred to were the wheels of oppression with their numerous spokes each representing the various forms oppression takes. Bayard Rustin practiced and taught the power of non-violent resistance. The "angelic troublemakers" throughout our history have stood up, spoken up, and laid down their bodies in the struggle to dismantle these wheels and prevent them from ever again trampling over the rights and the lives of people.

Following the legacy of non-violence, a new generation of committed and talented young activists has begun to change hearts and minds in the growing national movement for firearms safety. In a relatively brief time, they have scored some victories great and small.

In the aftermath of the tragic slaughter and injury of scores of students and educators at Marjory Stoneman Douglas High School on

February 14, 2018 in Parkland, Florida, students have engaged in massive school walkouts, and have attended national and regional rallies and marches. They have brought to the fore critical issues sparking discussions regarding the place of firearms in the society and the extent of the gun culture permeating our politics, our businesses, and our institutions.

Within one month of the Parkland shooting, the Florida legislature passed a modest bill signed into law by the governor. It raised the age to purchase any gun in the state to 21. Potential gun purchasers will now have to undergo a three-day waiting period, or until a background check is completed, whichever is longer. The law bans so-called "bump stocks" and other technologies that increase the speed of rifles.

The most controversial provision will allow school superintendents and local law enforcement to arm school personnel. The bill allocates $67. million to train and arm some employees on a voluntary basis, such as counselors, coaches, librarians – though not full-time teachers – in the use of firearms.

Legislators, by the narrowest of majorities, passed the bill despite a massive lobbying effort by the National Rifle Association for its defeat. Following its passage, the NRA filed a lawsuit against the state of Florida claiming:

> "This bill punishes law-abiding gun owners for the criminal acts of a deranged individual," argued executive director of the NRA Institute for Legislative Action Chris W. Cox. "Securing our schools and protecting the constitutional rights of Americans are not mutually exclusive" (Almasy, 2018).

The NRA was founded in 1871 primarily as a group for hunting and shooting enthusiasts. During the 1960s, in the wake of assassination of President John F. Kennedy, his brother Robert F. Kennedy, and the Reverend Dr. Martin Luther King Jr., the US Congress passed the Gun Control Act of 1968. The act regulated the firearms industry and owners by prohibiting the transfer of firearms over state borders except among licensed manufacturers, dealers, and importers.

The enforcement arm of the government was expanded in 1972 when the US created the Bureau of Alcohol, Tobacco, and Firearms. To counter what the NRA perceived as the encroachment against the rights of the

Second Amendment, NRA board member, Harlon Carter, established a lobbying arm of the organization, the NRA Institute for Legislative Action. Today it functions as one of the most powerful and well-funded member- and corporate-supported lobbying groups in the country. (In his youth, Carter killed 15-year-old Ramón Casiano and was convicted of Casiano's murder. Later, the conviction was overturned.)

In the year 2016 alone, it spent $35,157,585. Coming in a distant second in lobbying spending was the US Chamber of Commerce at $29,106,034. According to the Center for Responsive Politics, the NRA spent $51,854,687 during the 2016 federal election cycle helping put Donald J. Trump in the Oval Office and other high-profile Republican NRA supporters in Congress. Overall, gun rights lobbies' spending far exceeds that of the organizations for common sense gun safety.

When calls ring out for responsible gun regulations, the NRA, for example, falls back on it old effective battle cry of "They're trying to take away your guns!" to instill fear as a clarion call for the troops to staff the battlements. These conspiracy warriors live and die by the motto that no regulation is good regulation.

As is common in political and corporate advertising – and as we have seen as well in the Russian hacking of our democratic institutions – the gun rights lobby, including the NRA, micro-targets audiences and sites most susceptible or potentially interested in its message and goals, and as a means of contradicting and mediating counter narratives. The gun lobby has trolled my own articles on firearms safety by unloading an entire series of announcements for readers to take actions against any regulations on the unlimited manufacture, sale, and use of these weapons great and small; to join the NRA and to contact members of Congress; to applying for a free map showing all the "Concealed Carry" municipalities across the country.

Though my Senior Editor has continually attempted to block these ads from appearing on The Good Men Project website, dedicated pro-gun propagandists, nonetheless, find ways of dumping their muck. Possibly, though, we may be seeing the first tiny glimpses of hope for common sense comprehensive regulations. Stemming from the passion of the young activists from Marjorie Stoneman Douglas High School, increasing numbers of corporate sponsors are pulling their support from organizations like the NRA. Corporations include Avis Budget Group, Best Western, United Airlines, MetLife and Wyndham Worldwide. In addition, several local and national chain stores have recently restricted the selling of firearms. For example, Dick's Sporting Goods will no longer sell assault-style weapons and high capacity magazines, and it has raised the age to 21 for all other firearms. Walmart, which already has ceased selling assault weapons, like Dick's, has recently raised the age to 21 for other guns.

Selective states and local communities have been passing legislation, though this must happen on a national level, since individuals can still legally purchase firearms and accessories in many locations and carry them into places where they are outlawed. But possibly, we are seeing a clearing in the gun smoke coming on the horizon.

References

Almasy, S. (2018, March 9). NRA sues Florida to block part of new gun law. *CNN* online.

Center for Responsive Politics. (2016). Political nonprofits: Top election spenders. Retrieved 9/9/2019, https://www.opensecrets.org/outsidespending/nonprof_elec.php?cycle=2016.

Gadoua, R. K. (2015, June 30). Gay civil rights activist, MLK mentor Bayard Rustin to be honored. *Washington Post*.

Chapter Six

Obama Did What He Could, Congress Must Run with Baton

I want to thank President Obama for his commitment and his passion in his long-standing attempts to reduce firearms violence and death in the United States while he served as our 44th President. After lobbying Congress throughout his presidency to pass common sense gun regulations, and finding consistent confrontation, inaction, and intransigence on the part of legislators, Mr. Obama announced that he would issue Executive Orders to expand background checks for certain buyers of firearms.

The Orders mandated that individuals "in the business of selling firearms" register as licensed gun dealers. This would close the so-called "gun show loophole" that had previously exempted small sellers like gun hobbyists and collectors from maintaining official sales records. In addition, the Orders would have increased funding for enforcement by hiring 200 new Bureau of Alcohol, Tobacco, Firearms, and Explosives agents and investigators, and $4 million to track illegal online firearms trafficking.

The President was, however, realistic that the initiatives would not by themselves solve the epidemic plaguing our nation. Speaking at a press conference on January 5, 2016, he conceded:

> We know we can't stop every act of violence, every act of evil in the world. But maybe we could try to stop one act of evil, one act of violence (Bradner & King, 2016).

For this reason, he continued to challenge national legislators: "But we also can't wait," Obama added. "Until we have the Congress that's in line with the majority of Americans, there are actions within my legal authority that we can take to help reduce gun violence and save more lives."

The reaction from Republican leaders was swift and predictable. House Speaker Paul Ryan expected that the president's Executive Order "will no doubt be challenged in the courts" and "can be overturned by a Republican President" (Bradner & King, 2016).

Most Republican presidential candidates in 2016 came out shooting through their mouths. For example, New Jersey Republican Governor Chris Christie called Obama a "petulant child," and continued: "This president wants to act as if he is a king, as if he is a dictator. [If the courts don't overturn his actions], I'm sure that ultimately the next president will make sure that he abdicates those extra constitutional actions" (Atkin, 2016).

According to then presidential hopeful Donald Trump: "I will veto, I will unsign that so fast. So fast." Republican Texas Senator and presidential candidate Ted Cruz called Obama's initiatives an "abuse" of executive power, and he vowed to repeal them when he is president. Florida Senator Marco Rubio also said he would repeal the orders if elected to the presidency. Presidential candidate Carly Fiorina seemed to enter the stratosphere in her reply: "It is delusional, dangerous, not to mention unconstitutional for Barack Obama and Hillary Clinton to continue to talk about climate change and gun control in the wake of a Paris terrorist attack, a San Bernardino terrorist attack, instead of talking about a plan to defeat [the Islamic State in Iraq and Syria]." Jeb exclamation mark Bush (JEB!) said: "I will fight as hard as I can against any effort by this president, or by any liberal that wants to take away people's rights that are embedded in the Bill of Rights, embedded in our Constitution."

Well, to those who talked about the Constitution and gun rights, I would remind them of a number of issues, the first being that Mr. Obama, being a Constitutional scholar, understood full well the legal implications of his actions. It never fails to amaze me, though, how some people spout the second clause of the Second Amendment, which reads: "...the right of the People to keep and bear arms shall not be infringed," while forgetting or discounting a key term in the first clause, "*well regulated.*"

No right granted in our founding documents – neither in the Declaration of Independence nor in our Constitution – and no matter how groundbreaking and progressive these documents were, they do not grant unfettered or limitless rights. Take for example one of the rights addressed in the First Amendment: the "freedom of speech."

Since its inclusion into the Constitution, legislators and the courts have defined the parameters of this right. The Supreme Court, for example, has ruled certain speech unconstitutional when it is "directed to inciting or producing ... imminent lawless action," and is "likely to incite or produce such action," *Brandenburg v. Ohio* (1969). The Court also ruled on the limits of perpetrating false statements when it defames an individual or individuals, *Gertz v. Robert Welch, Inc.* (1974).

We also have limits on what the courts define as obscenity, specifically that which lacks "serious literary, artistic, political, or scientific value": the so-called Three-Pronged Miller (*Miller v. California,* 1973) Test. The Courts have also placed severe restrictions (*New York v. Ferber,* 1982) on the production, distribution, and purchase of material deemed as "child pornography," even though some people have argued that this material should be protected under the First Amendment's "freedom of speech" clause.

The Supreme Court ruled in *Chaplinsky v. New Hampshire* (1942) as unconstitutional the use of "fighting words," which it defined as speech that "tend[s] to incite an immediate breach of the peace" by provoking a fight, so long as it is a "personally abusive [word] which, when addressed to the ordinary citizen, is, as a matter of common knowledge, inherently likely to provoke a violent reaction."

The Courts have also made it illegal to use other people's words and present them as one's own. In *Harper & Row v. National Enterprises* (1985) the Supreme Court has further validated copyright and trademark laws protecting individuals and companies of their "intellectual property." In addition, the Courts have ruled against companies for "false advertising" of their products.

Unfortunately, many gun rights advocates view any regulations as unacceptable and as a unconstitutional violation and abridgement of what for them is an unlimited scope of the Second Amendment.

Executive Orders

Mr. Obama issued 227 Executive Orders, or an average of 33 per each of his years in office. By comparison, George W. Bush issued 291 Orders (36 per year), Ronald Reagan issued 381 (48 per year), and Dwight D. Eisenhower issued an enormous 484 (81 per year). Though they received some push back, where were the large-scale cries criticizing King George W., King Ronnie, and King Ike? Where were the loud and bombastic calls for judicial actions to reverse these orders? Where were the accusations of unconstitutionality and abuse of executive powers in the release of their Executive Orders?

President Obama, in releasing his Executive Orders on firearms, provided a meager and restrained response to the explosive perennial problem of gun-related violence consuming our communities. The President, however, was acting within the tight constraints of our Constitution to do what he could before he left office to deal with what he decreed as the most vexing problem of his presidency. Congress, unfortunately, failed to take any significant action in passing common sense firearms safety legislation.

References

Atkin, E. (2016, January 5). GOP candidates reject Obama's tearful plea for gun control. *Think Progress* online.

Bradner, E., & King, G. (2016, January 5). Emotional Obama calls for 'sense of urgency' to fight gun violence. *CNN* online.

Chapter Seven

Gun Violence, Media, Community Mobilization, & Race

Mass shootings at predominantly white schools draw the most attention from journalists and lawmakers, but *The Post* has found that children of color are far more likely to experience campus gun violence – nearly twice as much for Hispanic students and three times for black students.

Cox & Rich, *The Washington Post*, March 23, 2018

While black students comprise 16.6% of the student school population of the United States, they experience school shooting at the rate of 34.1%. In most incidents where students of color were exposed to shootings in schools since 1999, the majority were targeted or in some cases accidental, rather than random (Cox & Rich, 2018).

The media now extensively cover the mass shootings with increasing rapidity in schools and some communities like the Las Vegas Country Music festival, exposing horrifying images on our TV screens and print outlets. Especially since the Columbine High School massacre in 1999, through Sandy Hook Elementary School and Marjorie Stoneman Douglas High School, parents and other advocacy groups, with the great infusion of courageous and committed young people, have stepped up and taken the lead in a newly energized movement for firearms safety regulations.

While black people comprise 14% of the total U.S. population, however, they are victims of more than 50% of all gun homicides. Of the average 11,000 --13,000+ people murdered each year with guns, black men are 13 times at greater risk than are white men (Henry J. Kaiser Foundation, 2017). Where are the media in exposing the violence in primarily communities of color? Where are the massive national marches against this violence? Where are the loud and coordinated legislative calls for stricter gun controls?

Our current times recall the early years of the HIV/AIDS epidemic in the 1980s when gay and bisexual men were considered as those primarily affected. It was a time of virtual silence by powerful government leaders and scientific researchers. One can reasonably argue that if most people with HIV/AIDS initially had been middle-class, white, suburban heterosexual males, rather than gay and bisexual males, trans people, people of color, working-class people, sex workers, drug users, and Haitian Americans, we would have immediately seen massive mobilization to defeat the virus.

Well, today, since white young men comprise most of the school shooters in primarily white middle-class schools and communities, we are finally seeing massive mobilization to deal with the problem of gun violence. Stigmatized and marginalized groups, however, live with the constant reality of arbitrary and unprovoked systematic violence directed against them simply on the basis of their social identities. The intent of this xenophobic (fear and hatred of anyone or anything seeming "foreign") violence is to harm, humiliate, and destroy the "other" for the purpose of maintaining hierarchical power positions and attendant privileges of the dominant group over minoritized groups.

On February 26, 2012, George Zimmerman, a neighborhood watch leader in Sanford, Florida, shot and killed 17-year-old Trayvon Martin. Martin was walking on the sidewalk talking on a cell phone to his girlfriend and carrying a can of iced tea and a small bag of Skittles when Zimmerman confronted and shot him, and then he claimed self-defense. By most reports, Martin's "crime" was walking while being black in a predominantly white gated community visiting family and friends. His stigmata included his black skin and his youth while wearing a "hoody."

Black parents from all walks of life throughout the country engage with their children in what they refer to as "the talk" once they reach the age of 13 or 14 instructing them how to respond with calm if ever confronted by police officers. Parents of these young people know full well the stigmata embedded into their children by a racist society marking them as the expression of criminality, which perennially consigns them to the endangered species list.

In the wake of the killing of Trayvon Martin, 32-year-old Iraqi American Shaima Alawadi was the victim of a brutal hate-inspired murder in her San Diego, California home. On March 24, 2012, Alawadi's eldest daughter, Fatima al-Himidi, found Alawadi "drowning in her own blood," beaten with a tire iron. A note near Alawadi bloodied body read, "Go back to your country, you terrorist."

We witnessed the brutal police chokehold deaths of Eric Garner and George Floyd, the multiple-bullet police killings of Michael Brown, Tamir Rice, and Stephon Clark, the vigilante death of Trayvon Martin, the execution-style murders of three Muslim students in North Carolina – Deah Shaddy Barakat, a dental student, his wife, Yusor Mohammad Abu-Salha, and her sister, Razan Mohammad Abu-Salha – the destruction by arson of a building at the Islamic Institute in Houston, Texas, and the ever-increasing number of murders of primarily trans women of color.

And these are merely just a few of the most visible examples of this form of violence against unarmed members of stigmatized groups, primarily people of color. Earlier we witnessed the brutal attacks on Rodney King in Los Angeles, the barbarous slaying of James Byrd, Jr. in Jasper, Texas, and the fierce rape and murder of Cherise Iverson, a 7-year-old girl in a Las Vegas casino bathroom.

We must not and cannot dismiss these incidents as simply the actions of a few disturbed and sadistic individuals or to a limited number of "bad cops," for oppression exists on multiple levels in multiple forms. The killers live in a society that subtly and not-so-subtly promotes intolerance, spreads stereotypes, imposes stigmata, and perpetuates violence and the threat of violence. These incidents must be seen as symptoms of larger systemic national problems.

In these times of declining social mobility, and as the gap between the rich and the poor ever widens, dominant groups attempt to divide the dispossessed by pointing out scapegoats to blame. For example, vigilantes sometimes calling themselves members of the so-called "Minutemen" movement target and hunt down anyone suspected of entering this country undocumented. We are thus living in an environment in which property rights hold precedence over human rights. Metaphorically, oppression operates like a wheel with many spokes. If we work to dismantle only one or a few specific spokes, the wheel will continue to roll over people.

In the final analysis, whenever anyone of us is diminished, we are all demeaned, when anyone or any group remains institutionally and socially stigmatized, marginalized, excluded, or disenfranchised, when violence comes down upon any of us, the possibility for authentic community cannot be realized unless and until we become involved, to challenge, to question, and to act in truly transformational ways.

References

Cox, J. W., & Rich, S. (2018, March 23). Scared by school shootings. *Washington Post* online.

Henry J. Kaiser Family Foundation. (2017). Number of deaths due to firearms per 100,000 population by race/ethnicity. Retrieved 9/9/2019, https://www.kff.org/other/state-indicator/firearms-death-rate-by-raceethnicity/?currentTimeframe=0&selectedDistributions=white--black&sortModel=%7B%22colId%22:%22Location%22,%22sort%22:%22asc%22%7D

Chapter Eight

Sexual & Gun Violence Normalized

We saw a virtual bumper crop of headline stories in 2018 harvested in the fields of electronic and print media. President Trump's former campaign chair was tried and found guilty of 8 counts of felony tax fraud, and the president's long-time lawyer and "fixer" pleaded guilty to 8 counts of violating campaign finance laws. Hurricane Lane flooded the Hawaiian Islands with record-setting torrents, while back on the Mainland, western fires swallowed thousands of acres of forests and structures as the east sweltered in much-above-average temperatures for the last week of August.

Documentary images broadcast on TV and newspapers throughout the 50th anniversary of historic demonstrations and general melee outside and within the 1968 National Democratic Presidential Convention in Chicago. Reports indicated that over 500 children forcibly separated by I.C.E. officials under the Trump administration had still not been reunited with their parents who had come into the U.S. to seek refugee status after fleeing their violence-plagued Central American home countries. Vietnam War hero and long-time Congressional legislator, John McCain, succumbed in his battle with brain cancer.

A 24-year-old white gunman sprayed bullets into a crowd of contestants at a gaming tournament in Jacksonville, Florida in the 28th multiple shooting incident by August 26, 2018 leaving 11 injured and killing three, including the perpetrator.

An investigative report showed clear evidence that literally hundreds of Catholic priests in Pennsylvania sexually molested thousands of young people during the past decades while the Church hierarchy either ignored the incidents or simply transferred abusive priests to other parishes. An influential Catholic Bishop accused Pope Francis of engaging in an active coverup and demanded the Pope's resignation (Los Angeles Times Editorial Board, 2018).

But throughout this heavy harvest, the main story leading most broadcast news and placed above the fold on newspapers focused on the down-to-up-then-down-again positioning of the flag on the White House flagpole after the announced death of John McCain. The flag first appeared at half-staff immediately following the announcement but had been raised to full-staff the morning after. The American Legion stepped in to denounce the president's disgraceful conduct and disrespect for the Senator who gave his life in the service of the nation.

Where, however, is the sense of urgency and outrage by the continual barrage of priestly sexual assault? And where is the sense of urgency and outrage by the continual barrage of gun violence that plagues our nation? Where are the legislative reforms that can begin to stem the tide? Our nation has become so desensitized to violence that it now normalized to the same extent as daily local and national weather forecasts.

Some forms of desensitization serve beneficial and progressive functions. Seeing a multiracial couple or two people of the same sex walking lovingly hand-in-hand together down the sidewalk once deeply triggered people's biases and fears. While for some people this is still the case, for a great many more, the vision has become normalized in their lives. Unfortunately, however, many people and politicians have become desensitized to the day-to-day sexual and gun violence, which has allowed it to reach epidemic proportions. Young people generally now expect gun violence to touch their lives if it has not already done so.

The media and the public seem to have limited attention spans. Reports of the April 20, 1999 shooting massacre at Columbine High School in Colorado, the December 12, 2012 murders of elementary-age students and their teachers in Newtown Connecticut, and the 2002 priest sex scandal and coverup by the Boston Catholic Archdiocese shocked and captured the attention of a frightened and enraged nation. Soon afterward, however, the media took us onto the next big story, and the process continually repeated itself. Each time, thereafter, when the media report incidents of sexual or gun violence, the time frame grows increasing shorter with other stories tending to drown them out. (Except when the heroic student survivors and activists at Marjorie Stoneman Douglas High School grabbed the bullhorn and the public's attention and unleashed a movement for responsible gun reform along the way.)

Rather than following each shiny object Tweet of a distracting and obviously deranged Donald Trump in the Oval Office, the media and, most importantly, we the people should have focused our energy and commitment to pressuring our so-called law makers in tackling the important problems facing our country in the absence of presidential leadership. Gun violence on average takes 33,000 lives each year with 11,000+ as a result of murder and another 22,000 in accidents and suicides. Priests continue to molest young parishioners as the coverups continue.

We must re-sensitize ourselves and our nation to the scope of the problems. We must de-normalize the scourge of sexual and gun violence and normalize peace.

References

Los Angeles Times Editorial Board. (2018, September 13). The pope needs to clear the air over cover-ups in the Catholic Church–including about his own conduct. *Los Angeles Times* online.

Chapter Nine

Teachers Bearing Arms Makes No Sense

When billionaire philanthropist, Betsy DeVos, appeared in front of congressional legislators during her confirmation hearings as then President-elect Donald Trump's nominee for Secretary of the Department of Education, Democratic Senator Chris Murphy of Connecticut asked whether firearms should be allowed in schools as a strategy in protecting students. Rather than ruling it out, she answered: "I think that's best left to locales and states to decide."

When pressed further to elaborate, she referred to an earlier remark by Republican Senator Mike Enzi of Wyoming who mentioned an elementary school in Wapiti, Wyoming that erected a fence to protect students from wildlife. "I think probably there, I would imagine that there's probably a gun in the school to protect from potential grizzlies," DeVos said.

Well, aside from the possibility of arming bears, she later advocated for the bearing of arms for classroom teachers. She proposed using Department of Education funds to purchase guns and to cover the costs of firearms training for teachers as a tactic in reducing school gun violence (Ganim, Hansler, & Sullivan, 2018).

Following the deadly shooting massacre on February 14, 2018 at Marjorie Stoneman Douglas High School, and after meeting with survivors – including teachers, students, and parents – Trump placed DeVos in charge of heading a commission on school safety. As typical as it was in the Trump administration, Betsy DeVos, who came to her position with virtually no experience and knowledge of public education policy, pedagogy, and practices, chose commission members who had virtually no experience and knowledge of gun violence prevention.

During and following her congressional confirmation hearings, DeVos displayed her utter lack of qualifications and her contempt for public education. As a private citizen, she advocated for a voucher system that would divert funding from public schools to private and parochial schools and give greater emphasis on for-profit charter schools. She was then charged with plagiarism (Flores, 2017).

During her interview with Lesley Stahl on a March 12, 2018 CBS "60 Minutes" segment, when asked about her thoughts about school funding, she responded: "We should be funding and investing in students, not in school buildings, not in institutions, not in systems."

Several civil rights groups sued DeVos for revoking Title IX guidelines that help protect college survivors who report sexual assault. She had consistently reversed civil and human rights Obama-era protections for trans school students. On "60 Minutes," regarding her position on arming teachers in schools, she stated that "I hesitate to think of my first-grade teacher, Mrs. Zorhoff, I couldn't ever imagine her having a gun." Evidently, however, she not only imagined but advocated for current teachers to pack heat.

If she had listened to advice given by Douglas High School students and many others in the field of gun safety, rather than jumping to the beckoned call of the NRA and firearms manufacturers, she would cease trying to fight guns with more guns. Rather, she needed to advocate for common-sense gun safety legislation. But owing to long-held positions and the political climate, the chance of that Congress or the current one allowing proposed legislation to come to the floor is merely a pipe dream until and unless we change the composition of both houses in Washington, D.C. and in the State Houses throughout the country with solid majorities of gun safety advocates. Even then, it would be a steep climb.

Public schools continue to eliminate after-school programs and arts and humanities educational programs due to raising costs and reduced funding. Teachers on average spend hundreds of dollars each year out of their own pockets to help provide students with basic school supplies. Diverting funding from needed programs into arming teacher is a tactic that diverts us from the actual issue and the actual problem that there are simply too many legally obtained firearms in the United States that no amount of packing by teachers will alleviate or even reduce. In fact, it is likely to make it worse.

And to paraphrase political strategist James Carville, "It's the guns, stupid."

References

Flores, R. (2017, February 1). Former education secretary talks Betsy DeVos, plagiarism charges. *CBS News* online.

Ganim, S., Hansler, J., & Sullivan, K. (2018, August 23). Trump admin disputes NYT report on Education Department plan to arm teachers. *CNN* online.

Section Two

God

Chapter Ten

Patriarchy, Religion, & Christian Privilege

Conservative Evangelical Christians and other anti-choice and anti-LGBTQ zealots were downright giddy and literally ecstatic during the four years of the Trump administration over the possibility of finally receiving some of the promised dividends for selling their souls to the Devil in sacrificing all their "deeply held religious beliefs" by standing with Donald Trump throughout his unambiguously morally-reprehensible actions and policy directives.

They stood with him from his destructive and epithet-laden Tweets, to his promise of constructing a wall on our southern border that "Mexico will pay for," to the Access Hollywood tape, to revelations of his payoffs to quiet a porn star, to separating babies and young children from their parents and putting them in cages.

Throughout Trump's bullying candidacy to his plowing into the White House, his expectant base of supporters ran ahead like the excited sprinters in the annual Running of the Bulls in Pamplona, all with the hoped-for remuneration of Trump packing the judicial branch with decidedly right-wing judges and "justices."

The wall with Mexico was merely one of the many structures Trump promised to build. When he asserted during the campaign to punish women who have abortions and their doctors who perform them, he was figuratively walling-off women from their reproductive rights. By committing to reconstruct the Supreme Court with an untra-conservative majority and promising to reverse both *Roe v. Wade* and marriage equality, he gave social conservatives the vision of seeing a gigantic concrete and barbed-wire structure suspended high into the Heavens separating women and LGBTQ people from their bodies and from their civil rights, and, certainly, from their humanity. If Trump had actually fulfilled all his promises, the impact on religious conservatives would have even wider-ranging implications.

Burwell v. Hobby Lobby, 2014

> The owners of the businesses have religious objections to abortion, and according to their religious beliefs the four contraceptive methods at issue are abortifacients.
>
> Justice Samuel Alito, in the majority opinion,
> *Burwell v. Hobby Lobby.*

We can add "Justice" Samuel Alito, "Justice" Anthony Kennedy, "Justice" John Roberts, "Justice" Clarence Thomas, and last, but certainly not least, "Justice" Antonin Scalia to an oxymoronic list since this Supreme Court decision amounted to anything but justice. The five *men* voting in the majority denied the rights of women, most particularly working-class women employees at "closely-held" (family owned with a limited number of shareholders) for-profit corporations, which includes most U.S. corporations, control over their reproductive freedoms generally extended to women at other companies.

The case involved the owning families of the national chain of craft stores, Hobby Lobby, plus a Christian bookstore chain, and Conestoga, a Mennonite family-owned woodworking company who claimed and won the argument that the 2010 Affordable Care Act, and in particular, a few specific contraceptive devises covered by health insurance companies, violates the Religious Freedom Restoration Act of 1993 stating that "Government shall not substantially burden a person's exercise of religion ... . " The decision followed former 2012 presidential candidate Willard Mitt Romney's assertion during a campaign stop at the Iowa State Fair that "Corporations are people my friend," and clearly shows that million- and billion-dollar corporate families certainly exist more humanly (they are more of a person) and have more rights than workers.

When patriarchal social and economic systems of male domination attempt to keep women pregnant and taking care of children, they can restrict their entry, or at least their level and time of entry, into the workplace, and ensure women's dependence on men economically and emotionally. As women produce more and more children, expanding numbers of little consumers emerge to contribute to the capitalist system ever increasing profits for owners of business and industry. The patriarchal imperative to control women's and LGBTQ bodies amounts to imperatives to control their minds and life choices. And when patriarchal social and family structures converge with patriarchal religious systems, which reinforce strictly defined gender hierarchies of male domination, women and girl's oppression and the oppression of those who transgress sexuality- and gender-based boundaries became inevitable.

Polytheism and Monotheism

Many ancient and non-Western cultures – including, for example, Hindu, most Native American, Mayan, and Incan cultures – base their religions on polytheism (multiple deities). In general, these religious views seem to attribute similar characteristics to their gods. Particularly significant is the belief that the gods are actually created, and they age, give birth, and engage in sex. Some of these gods even have sexual relations with mortals. The universe is seen as continuous, ever-changing, and fluid. These religious views often lack rigid categories, particularly true of gender categories, which become mixed and often ambiguous and blurred. For example, some male gods give birth, while some female gods possess considerable power.

In contrast, monotheistic Abrahamic (Judaism, Christianity, Islam) religions view the Supreme Being as without origin, for this deity was never born and will never die. This Being, viewed as perfect, exists completely independently from human beings and transcends the natural world. In part, such a Being has no sexual desire, for sexual desire, as a kind of need, is incompatible with this concept of perfection. This accounts for the strict separation between the Creator and the created. Just as the Creator is distinct from *His* creation, so too are divisions between the Earthly sexes in the form of strictly defined gender roles. This distinction provides adherents to monotheistic religions a clear sense of their designated *socially constructed* roles: the guidelines they need to follow in relation to their God and to other human beings.

Since the United States is majority Christian in all its many sects and denominations, and all five men voting in the Supreme Court majority follow some form of Christianity, I have extracted just a few of the many examples of what the Christian Testaments say about women. (As an aside, if one shops at Hobby Lobby, when checking out at the cash register, one often sees for sale a small tin of candy called "Testamints." Really, no joke.)

Ephesians 5:21: Be subject to one another out of reverence for Christ. 5:22: Wives, be subject to your own husbands as to the Lord. 5:23: For the man is the head of the woman, just as Christ also is the head of the church. Christ is, indeed, the Savior of the body. 5:24: but just as the church is subject to Christ, so must women be subject to their husbands in everything.

1 Timothy 2:11: A woman must be a learner, listening quietly and with due submission .... 2:13: For Adam was created first, and Eve afterwards. 2:14: and it was not Adam who was deceived; it was the woman who, yielding to deception, fell into sin. 2:15: Yet she will be saved through motherhood – if only women continue in faith, love, and holiness, with a sober mind.

Whatever the intended purpose (which seems quite clear) of these texts and multiple others throughout scriptures, individuals, institutions, and entire societies have taken them to justify and rationalize the marginalization, harassment, denial of rights, and persecution of women and girls over the ages.

Christian Privilege

As spring peers forth from the soil and tree limbs, the annual Easter Egg Roll, sponsored by the President of the United States and the First Lady, thrills elementary and pre-school age children each year. Also, in school classrooms throughout the country, students and their teachers dip hardboiled eggs into brightly colored dyes, and display Easter eggs of pink, yellow, blue, green, red, and lavender. Some students adhere bunny, baby chick, rainbow, or angel decals to their Easter eggs. Some paint flowers or clouds; some sprinkle glitter of silver or gold.

An excitement wafts through the classroom as students imagine sharing their treasures with parents or caregivers, as teachers reward the good work of their young charges with delicious gleaming chocolate bunnies. A palpable exhilaration fills the air in anticipation of Easter Sunday as children adorn classroom bulletin boards with images of the season.

Many people (most likely the majority) consider these events, played out in Washington, DC and in some schools in the United States, as normal, appropriate, and joyous seasonal activities. Upon critical reflection, however, others experience them as examples of institutional (governmental and educational) (re)enforcements of dominant Christian standards and what is referred to as "Christian privilege" and "Christian hegemony," though presented in presumably secularized forms. They represent some of the ways in which the dominant group (in this instance, Christians) reiterates its values and practices while marginalizing and subordinating those who do not adhere to Christian faith traditions.

As an educator of pre-service teachers in the university, I am gratified to find that an ever-increasing number of Colleges of Education include instruction on issues of power and privilege related to our socially constructed identities. We know that teachers must thoroughly come to terms with their social positions ("positionalities"), the intersectional ways in which they are privileged as well as how they have been the targets of systemic inequities, and the impact this makes on their students.

Alexis de Tocqueville, French political scientist and diplomat, traveled across the United States for nine months between 1831–1832 conducting research for his epic work, *Democracy in America* (1850/1956). He was astounded to find a certain paradox: on one hand, he observed that the United States promoted itself around the world as a country separating "church and state" (which itself is a Christian term since primarily Christians refer to their houses of worship as "churches"), where religious freedom and tolerance were among its defining tenets, but on the other hand, he witnessed that: "There is no country in the world where the Christian religion retains a greater influence over the souls of men than in America."

He answered this apparent contradiction by proposing that in this country with no officially-sanctioned governmental religion, denominations were compelled to compete with one another and promote themselves to attract and keep parishioners, thereby making religion even stronger. While the government was not supporting Christian denominations and churches, *per se*, religion to Tocqueville should be considered as the first of their *political* institutions since he observed the enormous influence Christian denominations had on the political process.

Though he favored U.S. style democracy, he found its major limitation to be in its stifling of independent thought and independent beliefs. In a country that promoted the notion that the majority rules, this effectively silenced minorities by what Tocqueville termed the "tyranny of the majority." This is a crucial point because in a democracy, without specific safeguards of minority rights – in this case minority religious rights – there is a danger of religious domination or tyranny over religious minorities and non-believers. The majority, in religious matters, have historically been adherents to mainline Protestant Christian denominations who often imposed their values and standards upon those who believed otherwise.

Social theorist, Gunnar Myrdal, traveled throughout the United States during the late 1940s examining U.S. society following World War II, and he discovered a grave contradiction or inconsistency, which he termed "an American Dilemma." He found a country, founded on an overriding commitment to democracy, liberty, freedom, human

dignity, and egalitarian values, coexisting alongside deep-seated patterns of racial discrimination, privileging white people, while subordinating people of color. While racism continues, this contradiction has
been powerfully reframed for contemporary consideration by religious
scholar, Diana Eck (2001):

> The new American dilemma is real religious pluralism, and it poses chal-
> lenges to America's Christian churches that are as difficult and divisive as
> those of race. Today, the invocation of a Christian America takes on a new set
> of tensions as our population of Muslim, Hindu, Sikh, and Buddhist neigh-
> bors grows. The ideal of a Christian America stands in contradiction to the
> spirit, if not the letter, of America's foundational principle of religious free-
> dom (p. 46).

Dominant group power and control is maintained and strengthened
by "hegemony" (Gramsci, 1971), which describes the ways in which the
dominant group, in this case Christians in general and predominantly
mainline Protestants, successfully disseminate *its* particular form of
social reality and social vision in such a manner as to be accepted as
common sense, as "normal," as universal – even though only an estimated 30% of the world's inhabitants are Christian (Smith & Harter,
2002) – and as representing part of the natural order, even at times by
those who are marginalized, disempowered, or rendered invisible by it
(Tong, 1989). According to Weinbaum (2009), "[H]egemony is a means
for social control, not through overt force, but rather through covert tactics, dictating society's norms" (p. 99). This religious hegemony maintains the marginality of already marginalized religions, faiths, and
spiritual communities. Beaman (2003) wrote that "the binary opposition of sameness/difference is reflected in Protestant/minority religion
in which mainstream Protestantism is representative of the 'normal'"
(p. 321).

A form of hegemony is "Christian hegemony," which can be
define as the overarching system of advantages bestowed on Christians.
It is the institutionalization of a Christian norm or standard, which
establishes and perpetuates the notion that all people are or should be
Christian thereby privileging Christians and Christianity, and exclud-
ing the needs, concerns, ethnic, religious, cultural practices, and life

experiences of people who are not Christian. Often overt, though at times subtle, Christian hegemony is oppression by intent and design, but also it comes in the form of neglect, omission, erasure, and distortion (Blumenfeld, 2006, p, 196).

In the service of hegemony is what is termed "discourse," which includes the ideas, written expressions, theoretical foundations, and language of the dominant culture. These are implanted within networks of social and political control, described by Foucault (1980) as "regimes of truth," which function to legitimize what can be said, who has the authority to speak and be heard, and what is authorized as true or as *the* truth.

The concept of oppression, then, constitutes more than the cruel and repressive actions of individuals upon others. It often involves an overarching system of differentials of social power and privilege by dominant groups over subordinated groups based on ascribed social identities or social group status. And this is not merely the case in societies ruled by coercive or tyrannical leaders, but also occurs even within the day-to-day practices of contemporary democratic societies (Young, 1990).

Depending on our multiple identities, society grants us simultaneously a great array of privileges while marginalizing us based solely on these identities. Several researchers have developed extensive lists (white, male, heterosexual, cisgender) charting the benefits and privileges accorded to individuals within differing dominant identity categories.

Based on Peggy McIntosh's (1988) pioneering investigations of white and male privilege, we can, by analogy, understand Christian privilege as constituting a seemingly invisible, unearned, and largely unacknowledged array of benefits accorded to Christians, with which they often unconsciously walk through life as if effortlessly carrying a knapsack tossed over their shoulders. This *system* of benefits confers dominance on Christians while subordinating members of other faith communities as well as non-believers. These systemic inequities are pervasive throughout the society. They are encoded into the individual's consciousness and woven into the very fabric of our social institutions, resulting in a stratified social order privileging dominant ("agent") groups while restricting and disempowering subordinate ("target") groups (Bell, 1997; Miller, 1976). In keeping with McIntosh's (1988) inventory outlining the manifestations of white privilege, authors have developed parallel lists summarizing overarching examples of Christian privilege (see e.g., Clark, Vargas, Schlosser, & Alimo, 2002; Schlosser, 2003). As Clark et al. (2002) assert:

> [T]he fact remains that all Christians benefit from Christian privilege regardless of the way they express themselves as Christians in the same way that all White people benefit from White privilege (p. 12 of manuscript version).

As there is a spectrum of Christian denominations and traditions, so too is there a hierarchy or continuum of Christian privilege based on 1) historical factors, 2) numbers of practitioners, and 3) degrees of social power. In this regard, in a United States context, though the gap in privilege between Christian denominations is apparently shrinking, white, mainline Protestant denominations may still have some greater degrees of Christian privilege, relative to some minority Christian denominations, for example, African American, Latinx, Asian American churches, Amish, Mennonites, Quakers, Seventh-Day Adventists, Jehovah's Witnesses, Eastern and Greek Orthodox, adherents to Christian Science and to the Church of Jesus Christ of Latter-Day Saints, and still in some quarters, to Catholics.

By "unpacking" the knapsack of privilege (whether Christian, white, male, heterosexual, cisgender, owning class, temporarily able bodied, English as first-language speakers, adult, and others) is to become aware and to develop critical consciousness of its existence and how it impacts the daily lives of both those with and those without this privilege.

Though we can never fully quantify privilege, by discarding the bifurcated binary perspective while charting privilege along a continuum considering context and identity intersectionality, we will come to a fuller and deeper awareness of issues of power and privilege, marginalization, and oppression as we work toward a more socially just society and world.

References

Beaman, L. G. (2003). The myth of pluralism, diversity, and vigor: The constitutional privilege of Protestantism in the United States and Canada. *Journal for the Scientific Study of Religion, 42*(3), 311–325.

Bell, L. A. (1997). Theoretical foundations for social justice education. In M. Adams, L. A. Bell & P. Griffin (Eds.), *Teaching for diversity and social justice* (pp. 3–15). New York: Routledge.

Blumenfeld, W. J. (2006). Christian privilege and the promotion of "secular" and not-so "secular" mainline Christianity in public schooling and the larger society. *Equity and Excellence in Education, 39*(3), 195–210.

Clark, C., Vargas, M. B., Schlosser, L. Z., & Alimo, C. (2002). Diversity initiatives in higher Education: It's not just "Secret Santa" in December: Addressing educational and workplace climate issues linked to Christian Privilege [Electronic version]. *Multicultural Education, 10*(2), 52–57.

Eck, D. L. (2001). *A new religious America: How a "Christian country" has now become the world's most religiously diverse nation*. New York: HarperCollins.

Foucault, M. (1980). *The history of sexuality, Part 1* (R. Hurley, Trans.). New York: Vintage Books.

Gramsci, A. (1971). *Selections from the prison notebooks* (Q. Hoare & G. N. Smith, Trans.). New York: International Publishers.

McIntosh, P. (1988). White privilege and male privilege: A personal account of coming to see correspondences through work in women's studies. *Working paper No. 189*. Wellesley, MA: Wellesley Center for Research on Women.

Miller, J. B. (1976). *Toward a new psychology of women*. Boston, MA: Beacon Press.

Myrdal, G. (1962). *An American dilemma: The Negro problem and modern democracy*. New York: Harper & Row.

Schlosser, L. Z. (2003). Christian privilege: Breaking a sacred taboo. *Journal of Multicultural Counseling and Development, 31*(1), 44–51.

Smith, D. J., & Harter, P. M. (2002). *If the world were a village: A book about the world's people*. Stanford, CA: Stanford University Press.

de Tocqueville, A. (1840/1956). *Democracy in America*. New York: The New American Library.

Tong, R. (1989). *Feminist thought: A comprehensive introduction*. Boulder, CO: Westview Press.

Weinbaum, L. M. (2009). Clash over the crosses: Las Cruces New Mexico – Preserving "Our cultural heritage" or maintaining Christian hegemony. In W. J. Blumenfeld, K. Y. Joshi, & E. E. Fairchild (Eds.). *Investigating Christian privilege and religious oppression in the United States* (pp. 97–111). Rotterdam, Netherlands: Sense Publishers.

Young, I. M. (1990). *Justice and the politics of difference*. Princeton, NJ: Princeton University Press.

Chapter Eleven

Christian Crusaders Carry and Shoot for Liberty

Liberty University, founded by late Southern Baptist pastor and tel-evangelist, Jerry Falwell, announced its precedent-setting plans to become the first U.S. university with its own National Rifle Association-compliant gun range facility. The university took this action just one year after the board of trustees approved a policy to allow students to carry concealed firearms on campus (Ambrosino, 2016).

Jerry Falwell Jr., then President of Liberty University in Lynchburg, Virginia, one year earlier urged all students at the school's *mandatory* convocation to apply for concealed-carry permits so they can proudly bear firearms around the campus. He said:

> "I've always thought that if more good people had concealed-carry permits, then we could end those Muslims before they walked in," he proclaimed to the loud unrestrained applause of students. "I just wanted to take this oppor-tunity to encourage all of you to get your permit. We offer a free course," he said. "Let's teach them a lesson if they ever show up here" (Badash, 2015).

Falwell acknowledged a large elongated protrusion in his trou-sers: "If some of those people in that community center [in California]

had what I have [a .25 caliber pistol] in my back pocket right now ... ,"
he said while students interrupted with even louder cheers and sustained clapping. "Is it illegal to pull it out? I don't know," he continued
while chuckling.

Falwell said he owns several shotguns, rifles, and pistols, which he
has kept on his farm for several years, and he confirmed that he was
given a license to carry a concealed weapon a year earlier. Later, Junior
clarified that "those Muslims" to whom he was referring represent
people like Syed Farook and Tashfeen Malik, the couple who shot and
killed 14 people in a San Bernardino, California office building during
a holiday party on December 2, 2015.

Junior took over as president of Liberty University in 2007 after the
passing of his controversial father, Jerry Falwell Sr., who founded the
conservative Christian institution in 1971.

"Carrying" To Its Logical Conclusions

So, what are the implications of students carrying concealed weapons
on the grounds of Liberty University, and on institutions of "higher
learning" throughout the United States? Let me count just some of
the ways:

1. More and more unauthorized deputies will engage in citizens'
   vigilante (in)justice by misappropriating the national security
   duties of local, municipal, state, and national governmental
   agencies.
2. Students will no longer have need of the previously dependable
   apple to entice professors to raise grades on their term papers.
3. Students will have increased options to end domestic quarrels or
   quell partners' threats of breakups.
4. Depressed students will have greater means of ending their pain.
5. Rather than simply giving professors nasty course evaluations
   on the many online sites, students will now effectively take out
   educators and spare future generations the torments of having to
   listen to their classroom chatter.

6. And of course, on a college campus or anywhere, firearms and alcohol always combine to produce pleasurable experiences.

But I would ask Falwell, if the historical Jesus were alive today, would he apply for a concealed-carry permit, or instead, would he accuse you of misinterpreting and thoroughly distorting his message? What do you think, Junior?

Fortunately, though, Junior will no longer have the option of influencing young minds. He handed in his resignation as Chancellor and President of Liberty University and from its Board of Directors in 2020 following discovery of a photo of himself, alcoholic drink in hand, with his arm around a woman who was not his wife while both wore unzipped pants. In addition, reports surfaced that he engaged in an alleged affair with his wife and another man (Whitford, 2020).

References

Ambrosino, B. (2016, December 9). Liberty University to build nation's first on-campus firing range. *Yahoo News* online.

Badash, D. (2015, December 5). Liberty University President: 'If More Good People' Had Concealed Guns, 'We Could End Those Muslims.' *New Civil Rights Movement* online.

Whitford, E. (2020). Jerry Falwell officially resigns. *Inside Higher Ed, 9/26/2020*

Chapter Twelve

Firearms Regulation Is a Moral Imperative

As I sit here sad and enraged on February 14, 2018 ironically on Valentine's Day while writing yet another commentary on the scourge of gun violence plaguing the United States mere hours after the horrific slaughter by a gun*man* who snuffed out the lives and futures of 17 people and injured another 15, some seriously at Marjory Stoneman Douglas High School in Parkland, Florida, I think once again that "it does *not* have to be this way!"

The shooter, though, a young man of 19 legally purchased an AR-15 semi-automatic rifle that another eight million residents of the U.S. also own, though he is not yet old enough to legally buy a can of beer. These types of rifles are made and used to assault people and not to assault Bambi.

Each year, the U.S. Centers for Disease Control and Prevention publish its National Vital Statistics Reports and finds that gun-related deaths have reached epidemic proportions in our country by snuffing out the lives of well over 30,000 people (with 1/3 homicides and the remainder suicides and accidents) and wounding many more annually. The gun safety group Brady: United Against Gun Violence found that on average, 310 people are shot in the United States every day with 100 dying. Seven children and teens are killed on average daily. Many of the guns used in these killings reach military level weapons power, guns which currently remain legal to purchase (Brady, 2019).

Today in the United States, there are approximately 120 firearms per 100 people. Our country ranks high when compared with 22 other wealthy industrialized nations in per capita gun-related deaths with 3.85 per 100,000 residents, compared, for example, with the United Kingdom at 0.07, Japan at 0.04, Germany at 0.12, Indonesia at 0.10, and Oman at 0.06 (Wikipedia, 2019).

A study by *The American Journal of Medicine* found that though the U.S. has half the population of the other 22 nations combined, it accounted for 82% of all gun deaths and 90% of all women killed by firearms. Also, 91% of youth under 14 who died by gun violence and 92% of young people between ages 15 and 24 killed by guns were in the United States (Preidt, 2016).

Long-time gun safety advocates and those newly on board have been calling for, pleading for lawmakers across the country to pass common-sense regulations on the manufacture, purchase, and owner-ship of firearms. In numerous instances, local, state, and national legis-lators have heeded the call by acting, but, paradoxically and callously, by making it *easier* for people to get their hands on these dangerous weapons of mass destruction.

Since the Newtown, Connecticut massacre on December 14, 2012 at Sandy Hook Elementary School, approximately 24 states have *extended* people's right to carry guns into public spaces such as bars, houses of worship, college campuses, and some businesses, and even into air-ports up to the TSA checkpoints. Some states, like former Speaker of the House Paul Ryan's Wisconsin, eliminated the 48-hour waiting period to buy a handgun. In Texas, students who are at least 21 may now carry guns anywhere on a university campus except into sports stadiums. And in Ohio, people have the right to carry firearms into daycare centers.

In December 2016, the Obama administration, released policy guidelines mandating that people receiving Social Security payments for severe mental illnesses and those found incapable of managing their finances undergo FBI's National Instant Criminal Background Checks if they request to purchase a weapon.

Congress, however, overturned the policy, primarily on party lines. President Trump signed into law a bill revoking Obama-era background checks for people with mental illnesses one month after taking office even though following every mass shooting during his presidency, he referred to these instances as a "mental health problem" as he did again after 17 students and their teachers were killed in Parkland, Florida.

After the horrific mass slaughter of outdoor country music concert goers by a gunman aiming a high powered rifle from a window in the Mandalay Bay Hotel in Las Vegas, gun rights advocates, and even many congressional legislators, believed they could, at last, shepherd through the legislative process in both chambers a basic regulation making it illegal to sell or use the so-called "bump stock" used by the shooter to increase the speed of some semi-automatic rifles.

Approximately 15 states began considering bump stock restrictions of their own, and the state of New Jersey and my home state of Massachusetts have enacted such laws. Prior to the Las Vegas shooting, New York and California had already imposed these restrictions. Finally in 2019, the Federal Bureau of Alcohol, Tobacco, Firearms, and Explosives and the Trump Administration officially banned these devises.

As Speaker of House of Representatives, Paul Ryan refused even to call for the creation and convening of a Select Committee on Gun Violence suggested by Democratic House Minority Leader Nancy Pelosi to "study and report back common sense legislation" to halt injuries and murders in this epidemic of mass shootings (Caygle & Schor, 2017). Trump in 2017 proposed cutting millions of dollars, amounting to 16%, from the National Criminal Records History Improvement Program and the NICS Act Record Improvement Program, which give states federal grants to improve reporting to the national background-check database.

So as the number of injuries and murders increase in mass and individual incidents of gun violence, while an estimated 90% of those polled want stepped-up background checks for all gun purchases, and while the highest percentage of U.S. residents ever recorded in a Quinnipiac survey in 2018 of 66 to 31% want *stricter* gun laws, support for universal background is 97 – 2%, including 97 – 3% among gun owners, and 67 – 29% for a nationwide ban on the sale of assault weapons:

> 83 - 14 percent for a mandatory waiting period for all gun purchases. It is too easy to buy a gun in the U.S. today, American voters say 67 - 3 percent. If more people carried guns, the U.S. would be less safe, voters say 59 - 33 percent. Congress needs to do more to reduce gun violence, voters say 75 - 17 percent (Quinnipiac University Poll, retrieved 2019).

Possibly when we as a collective nation begin to love young people more than we love guns, when we as a collective nation begin to love all our people more than we love guns and more than we love supporting gun manufactures and sellers who love money most of all, that is when we might pass gun safety laws!

The shooting in this Parkland, Florida High School was the 18th school shooting between January 1 and February 14, 2018, at least the 273rd school shooting overall, and the 1,607th mass shooting between the Sandy Hook school massacre and the one at Parkland. Comprehensive common-sense regulations for firearms safety are not simply and only political issues. They are moral imperatives! And let's not forget that the founders included the phrase "well regulated" in the Second Amendment.

References

Brady. (2019). The facts that make us act. Retrieved 9/9/2019, https://www.bradyuni ted.org/key-statistics

Caygle, H., & Schor, E. (2017, October 2). Pelosi calls on Ryan to form select committee to curb gun violence. *Politico* online.

Preidt, R. (2016, February 3). How U.S. gun deaths compare to other countries. *CBS News* online.

Quinnipiac University Poll on Guns, Retrieved 12/31/19, https://poll.qu.edu/natio nal/release-detail?ReleaseID=2521

Wikipedia. (2019). Estimated number of civilian guns per capita by country. Retrieved 9/9/2019, https://en.wikipedia.org/wiki/Estimated_number_of_civilian_guns_ per_capita_by_country

Chapter Thirteen

Ben Carson, Guns, & False Parallels to the Holocaust

Dr. Ben Carson, a Republican Party presidential candidate in 2016 and Secretary of the Department of Housing and Urban Development under the Trump administration, seemed obsessed with stretching himself into a pretzel to fabricate links between the conditions giving rise to and advancing the Nazi German Holocaust with conditions then enfolding within contemporary U.S.-America. For example, in Carson's published book, which he co-authored with his wife Candy, *A More Perfect Union: What We The People Can Do To Reclaim Our Constitutional Liberties* (2015), they discuss Nazi Germany's weapons confiscation policies. The Carsons argued that an armed citizenry is needed to protect the people against "tyrants" and "radicals."

They assert that our country must never impose restriction on firearms since "our founders recognized that 'we the People' could represent a significant fighting force if necessary to repel an invasion by foreign forces. They also knew that an armed population would discourage government overreach." The Carsons wrote:

The founders feared an overbearing central government might attempt to dominate the people and severely curtail their rights. This, in fact, is the primary reason that the Second Amendment was included in the Bill of Rights (2015, from Chapter 6, n.p.).

The Carsons anticipated that many people might charge that it is "ludicrous to imagine our federal government trying to seize unconstitutional power and dominate the people." By referring to James Madison, the Carsons said the founder "could foresee a day in America when radicals might assume power and try to impose upon America a different system of government." They continued, "His hope was that the establishment of such a different way of life would be difficult in America, because American citizens, having the right to keep and bear arms, would rebel."

And in this context, they referred to Adolf Hitler and Nazi Germany, writing how "German citizens were disarmed by their government in the late 1930s, and by the mid-1940s Hitler's regime had mercilessly slaughtered six million Jews and numerous others whom they considered inferior."

Only law-abiding citizens are affected by legislation imposing gun control. The criminals don't care what the law says, which is why they are criminals. Confiscating the guns of American citizens would violate the Constitution as well as rendering the citizenry vulnerable to criminals and tyrants (2015, n.p.).

Ben Carson stepped in it when Wolf Blitzer interviewed the candidate and former neurosurgeon on CNN by declaring that Jewish people under the Nazi regime might have prevented the Holocaust if they had been armed. Blitzer asked Carson: "Just to clarify, if there had been no gun control laws in Europe at that time, would 6 million Jews have been slaughtered?" (Associated Press, 2015).

Responding to Blitzer, Carson said: "I think the likelihood of Hitler being able to accomplish his goals would have been greatly diminished if the people had been armed. I'm telling you that there is a reason that these dictatorial people take the guns first."

Carson proclaimed to a standing ovation by a conservative crowd listening to his stump speech during a March 2014 event in New York, that according to the conservative website Breitbart TV, "Carson said the current state of our government and institutions are 'very much like Nazi Germany': You had the government using its tools to intimidate the population. We now live in a society where people are afraid to say what they actually believe." He blamed the U.S.'s Nazi-like conditions on so-called political correctness and government intimidation (Breitbart TV, 2014). And in a September 2014 interview with J. D. Hayworth of Newsmax, Carson advised people to read Hitler's manifesto, *Mein Kampf* (My Struggle), and also to read the works of Vladimir Lenin to draw their own parallels with President Obama and the United States (Tashmam, 2014).

Carson is *completely* misguided as are other anti-gun regulations activists regarding Hitler's actual policies. University of Chicago law professor Bernard Harcourt investigated this myth in his article published in the Fordham Law Review (Harcourt, 2004). He discovered that the Weimar Republic, the German government immediately preceding Hitler's, enacted *tougher* firearms restrictions than under the Nazi's. After its defeat in World War I, under the terms of the Treaty of Versailles, in 1919, the German legislature passed a law banning all private firearms, and the government confiscated guns already in circulation. According to Harcourt, however, "The 1938 revisions [signed by Hitler] completely deregulated the acquisition and transfer of rifles and shotguns, as well as ammunition."

Under this 1938 law, many additional categories of people, including Nazi party members, were excused from all gun ownership regulations, and the legal age to purchase firearms was lowered from 20 to 18. Also, the length of time the permits were in affect increased from one to three years. Yes, the law *did* prohibit Jews and other oppressed groups from firearms ownership, but the vast majority of Germans were free to purchase weapons.

In the past, Carson all but blamed the victims of tragic shooting for their own murders at the Emanuel African Methodist Episcopal Church in Charleston, South Carolina killing 9 parishioners, and at Umpqua Community College in Roseburg, Oregon also killing 9, by asserting that instead of merely succumbing to threats by shooters brandings firearms, people must stand up and aggressively confront shooters. Referring to the shooting in Oregon, Carson said:

> If everybody attacks that gunman, he's not going to be able to kill everybody. But if you sit there and let him shoot you one-by-one, you're all going to be dead. And, you know, maybe these are things that people don't think about. It's certainly something that I would be thinking about (CBS News, 2015).

Unfortunately, myths and untruths continue related to the supposed firearms restrictions for the majority of Christian Germans under the Third Reich.

References

Associated Press. (2015, October 9). Ben Carson tells Wolf Blitzer: Holocaust would have been "greatly diminished" if Jews had guns. Online. Retrieved 9/9/2019, https://www.hollywoodreporter.com/news/ben-carson-holocaust-greatly-diminished-830938.

Breitbart TV. (2014, March 12). Exclusive: Dr. Ben Carson: Our government is like 'Nazi Germany.' *Breitbart*, Retrieved 8/24/2021, https://www.breitbart.com/clips/2014/03/12/Exclusive-Dr-Ben-Carson-Our-Government-Is-Like-Nazi-Germany/

Carson, B., & Carson, C. (2015). *A more perfect union: What we the people can do to reclaim our constitutional liberties.* New York: Sentinel.

CBS News. (2015, October 7). Ben Carson defends comments about Oregon shooting. Online. Retrieved 9/9/2019, https://www.cbsnews.com/news/election-2016-gop-dr-ben-carson-gun-control/.

Harcourt, B. E. (2004). On gun registration, the NRA, Adolf Hitler, and Nazi gun laws: Exploding the gun culture wars (A call to historians). *Fordham Law Review, 73*(2), 653–680.

Tashman, B. (2014, September 9). Ben Carson: To know Obama, read 'Mein Kampf.' *Right Wing Watch*, a project of People for the American Way. Retrieved 9/9/2019, https://www.rightwingwatch.org/post/ben-carson-to-know-obama-read-mein-kampf/.

Section Three

Hypermasculinity

Chapter Fourteen

Patriarchy Still Alive and Functioning

What is patriarchy? A society is patriarchal to the degree that it promotes male privilege by being *male dominated, male identified,* and *male centered*. It is also organized around an obsession with control and involves as one of its aspects the oppression of women.

Allan G. Johnson, 1997, p. 5.

Friedrich Engels (1884) saw how economic developments encouraging the accumulation of private property required the fortification of the monogamous family to guarantee that men's property would be inherited by their biological heirs. Engels was the one of the first to argue that women's subordination was not the result of any biological dispositions, but rather, caused by "men's efforts to achieve their demands for control of women's labor and sexual faculties [which] have gradually solidified and become institutionalized in the nuclear family" (Holborn & Steel, 2012, n.p.).

If a patriarchal social and economic system of male domination can keep women pregnant and taking care of children following birth, they can restrict their entry, or at least their level and time of entry, into the workplace, and ensure women's dependence upon men economically and emotionally. As women produce more and more children, expanding numbers of little consumers emerge to contribute to the capitalist system ever increasing profits for owners of business and industry. The patriarchal system necessary to control women's bodies amounts to imperatives to control women's minds and life choices.

In addition, the family's incessant reification and promotion of hegemonic binary gender categories is now (partially) what drives families in the U.S. to ex-communicate their LGBTQ children and provides fuel for the socially conservative capitalist class to spread sexism, cissexism, and heterosexism because of capitalists' direct benefit from traditional gender roles rooted in the family-household system. Thus, when a patriarchal family structure converges with a patriarchal religious system, which itself reinforces and intensifies the enforcement of strictly defined gender hierarchies of male domination by restricting women's reproductive freedoms and decision making and ordaining requisite sexual and gender matrices, women's oppression and the oppression of those who transgress sexual- and gender-based boundaries became inevitable.

I define "sexism" as the overarching system of advantages bestowed on males. It is prejudice and discrimination based on sex, especially against females and intersex people, and is founded on a patriarchal structure of male dominance promoted through individual, institutional, social, and cultural systems.

Throughout history, examples abound of male domination over the rights and lives of women and girls. Men denied women the vote until women fought hard and demanded the rights of political enfranchisement, though women in some countries today still are restricted from voting by patriarchal systems; strictly enforced gender-based social roles mandated without choice that women's only option was to remain in the home to undertake cleaning and childcare duties; women were and continue to be by far the primary target of harassment, abuse, physical assault, and rape by men; women were and remain locked out of many professions; rules once required that women teachers relinquish their jobs after marriage in some countries; in fact, the institution of marriage itself was structured on a foundation of male domination with men serving as the so-called "head of the household" and taking on sole ownership of all property, thereby restricting these rights from women. In other words, women have been constructed as second-class and even third-class citizens, but through it all, women as a group have challenged the inequities and have pushed back against patriarchal constraints.

Though many people are fully aware of the continuing existence of sexism and male privilege, and they are working tirelessly for its eradication, many others, however, fail to perceive its harmful effects on themselves and others. This apparent invisibility of sexism and male privilege in many Western countries, in fact, not only fortifies but, indeed, strengthens this form of oppression and privilege by perpetuating patriarchal hegemony in such a way as to avoid detection. In other words, male dominance is maintained by its relative invisibility (though for many of us, it stands as blatantly obvious), and with this relative invisibility, privilege escapes analysis and scrutiny, interrogation and confrontation by many. Dominance is perceived as unremarkable or "normal," and when anyone poses a challenge or attempts to reveal its true impact and significance, those in the dominant group brand them as "subversive" or even "accuse" them of being "overly analytical." Possibly those who make these accusations are not themselves sufficiently analytical.

Toxic forms of hypermasculinity require the promotion and use of firearms to keep at bay the intensive psychosocial compulsive fear and dread of penetration from bullets, from homosexuals, from the female gaze since patriarchy promises males the right to the aggressive outward intrusive gaze, the right of penetration of "others." Laws are built upon and reflect the society in which they are meant to affect. Patriarchal individualistic societies oppress and inhibit women's reproductive freedoms, encourages the inequities in salaries between men and women, establishes and maintains the massive development of wealth for a very few while encouraging the enormous financial disparities between the very rich and everyone else, and many other issues.

That was then, but what about now?

I often hear some men and even some women claim that sexism is a thing of the past, that women have achieved the equality that was once denied them (at least in "Western" countries), that we live in a system of meritocracy where one's success in life is based solely on merit, work ethic, motivation, and abilities, rather than on our social identities or the stations of life to which we are born.

This was brought to light by a respondent to a commentary I wrote that appeared in my former university campus newspaper, the Iowa State *Daily*, titled "Awareness Rewards," in which I attempted to make visible the often-invisible condition of dominant group privilege, for example, male, white, heterosexual, and Christian.

Responding to my claim specifically of male privilege, the respondent flatly rejected the notion by providing examples allegedly showing otherwise:

> The idea that women are considered inferior is absurd in a nation where doors are opened for them from coast to coast, their meals and entertainment are paid by men eager to please them, they are the physical majority, they own the majority of wealth and control most of the rest, and they live longer because they have easier lives.

I would like to address these claims point by point.

Yes, men continue literally to open doors for women, and they often pay for their meals and entertainment. While this can in certain settings be regarded as a sign of politeness and admiration, does it actually indicate a true *respect* for women, and does this signify an equality among the sexes? I argue quite the contrary, that it represents, rather, a reification of socially constructed gender norms keeping a sexual hierarchy firmly in place, with men literally and figuratively on top, where men remain in control, and where women are expected to perform a dependent role.

The respondent also claimed that women are the physical majority. Yes, this is statistically true. I am afraid, however, that the respondent confuses "majority" in terms of numbers with dominance in terms of social power. For example, though black Africans numbered the vast majority under the corrupt apartheid system in South Africa, white South Africans held the social power to invoke and to maintain, for many years, their oppressive control.

In addition, do women in fact, as the respondent claims, "own the majority of wealth and control most of the rest." While women's annual salaries have grown over the past decades, and while many studies indicate that women have fared somewhat better, reports indicate that women continue to make substantially less than their male counterparts when performing similar roles in similar jobs. And this inequity is compounded substantially by the factor of "race" (Vagins, 2018).

In the respondent's claim that women live longer than men, while most comparative studies do indicate that women on average outlive men, I cannot see how this proves the absence of sexism and male domination. I would also like the respondent to validate the claim that women have "easier lives." Which criteria are this respondent considering?

The respondent continued: "Women are worshipped in this country, with beauty pageants to showcase them, like Miss America and Miss Universe. Where are the Mister America and Mister Universe pageants and who would watch them? Men knock themselves out in this country to find a good woman they can make the center of their world."

So, the question here arises, do these women's beauty pageants indicate a worshipping and veneration of women, or something else entirely? While pageants can offer several financial and career enhancing benefits to the women involved, let us be clear who and what is really being honored. Rather than considering women's beauty pageants as honoring women, I believe they further reinscribe gender roles by promoting socially constructed norms of beauty, which are exclusionary hegemonic ideologies in terms of body size and shape, standards for skin and hair type, and an idealized and circumscribed age range that acts to the detriment of all women. As such, beauty pageants remain a consumerist colonization of women's bodies for the edification and commodification of the objectifying male gaze.

The Social Construction of "Gender"

Within academia and activism, greater emphasis and discussion is centering on what has come to be called "queer studies," "queer theory," "critical trans politics," and "critical race theory" (areas of critical theory) where writers, educators, and students analyze and challenge current notions, categorizations, and repressive binary frames of sexuality, gender constructions, and race. Queer theory, for example, is founded on the principle that "identities" are not fixed or inflexible and are instead socially rather than biologically determined. Queer theorists have insisted that identities comprise many and varied components, and that it is inaccurate and misleading to collectively categorize people on the basis of one single element (for example, as "lesbian," "gay," "bisexual," "heterosexual," or as "woman," "man," and others).

Monique Wittig (1972), for example, asserted that the terms "woman" and "man" constitute *political* rather than eternal or essentialized categories. Preeminent scholar and social theorist Judith Butler (1990) addressed what she refers to as the "performativity of gender" in which "gender" is basically an involuntary reiteration or reenactment of established norms of expression, an act that one performs as an actor performs a script that was created before the actor ever took the stage. The continued transmission of gender requires actors to play their roles so that they become actualized and reproduced in the guise of reality, and in the guise of the "natural" and the "normal."

> The act that one does, the act that one performs, is, in a sense, an act that has been going on before one arrived on the scene. Hence, gender is an act, which has been rehearsed, much as a script survives the particular actors who make use of it, but which requires individual actors in order to be actualized and reproduced as reality once again (Butler, 1990. p. 272).

Several theorists argue that the notion of "gender" is a concept that is taught and learned and sustained in the service of maintaining positions of domination and subordination. Not only are the categories man/woman, heterosexual/homosexual and bisexual, and gender conforming/gender non-conforming binary frames inaccurate and constraining for the complexities and diversity of human bodies and lives, but they also leave no space for intersex people – the estimated one in 1500 to one in 2000 people born with either indeterminate or combined male and female sexed bodies – and transgender people. In the case of gender, the binary imperatives lock all people into rigid gender-based roles that inhibit creativity and self-expression, and therefore, we all have a vested interest in challenging and eventually obliterating the binaries.

I have heard some people refer to our current times as a "post-Feminist" era, where sexism and male privilege no longer impose major social barriers. They are referring to "Feminism," which can be defined as the cultural, political, economic, and civil rights movement for the advancement of equality and equity between the sexes.

For me this brings to mind a cleaver and I believe insightful bumper sticker produced by the National Association for Women: "I'll be Post-Feminist in the Post-Patriarchy." Unfortunately, however, the patriarchy is still alive and fully functioning.

References

Butler, J. (1990). *Gender trouble: Feminist and the subversion of identity.* New York: Routledge.

Engels, F. (1884). *The origin of the family, private property, and the state.* Zurich, Switzerland: Hollingen-Zurich.

Holborn, M., & Steel, L. (2012). *Families and households: AQA* Sociology Unit 1, New York: Harper Collins Publications.

Johnson, A. G. (1997). *The gender knot: Unraveling our patriarchal legacy,* Philadelphia, PA: Temple University Press.

Vagins, D. J. (2018). The simple truth about the gender pay gap. American Association of University Women. Retrieved 9/13/2019, https://www.aauw.org/research/the-simple-truth-about-the-gender-pay-gap/

Wittig, M. (1972). *The straight mind, and other essays.* Boston, MA: Beacon Press.

Chapter Fifteen

Parallels to Firearms Advocates

While Ben Carson as discussed in Chapter 13 previously seems intoxicated by the conspiratorial soup he ingested sparking hallucinatory comparisons between Nazi Germany and the United States, he does, in fact, parrot the Nazi Germany and contemporary U.S. connections: a primary argument spouted by what I am calling the "Pro-Firearms with No More Regulations Movement."

In my effort to better understand why the United States remains among the last of the more developed Western countries to resist instituting meaningful and appropriate gun control measures, I took the risk of engaging with a radical fringe of the movement on the Hypocrisy and Stupidity of Gun Control Advocates Facebook page. Virtually every responder to my comments lodged toxic personal attacks against my character, my masculinity, and my "using big words to impress," in addition to actual threats of violence against me. In addition, everyone engaged in binary, all or nothing, black or white thinking: total freedom and independence from government regulations v. governmental tyranny.

One person giving a more rational response on the theme connecting the U.S. to the Nazis and to Soviet-style Communism came from this man [I prefer to keep names confidential]:

> If you watch the History Channel, Hitler and many other dictators removed guns using the same thought process. 'Let's make our society safe by removing guns', it's logical and thoughtful. Not really, it's thought control. To (sic) many times the powers that want to remove an individuals (sic) right to self defense use this 'let's all get along' argument. I really don't think anyone who uses this argument really cares for the general populace.

Others who did not post abusive comments simply expressed their opinions on this topic by dispatching pictures, including the following:

One showed a picture of Adolph Hitler with the caption "To conquer a nation, first disarm its citizens." Another depicted a Nazi soldier shooting point blank at a male and female couple with the caption: "Gun control did this."

A third picture led with the statement above pictures of Washington, Jefferson, Madison, and Hamilton in all capital letters: "THESE MEN SUPPORT YOUR RIGHT TO BEAR ARMS:" followed by: "THESE MEN OPPOSE IT:" with pictures of Hitler, Stalin, Castro, Amin, Lenin, and Obama.

[Not a] Conclusion

Literally hundreds of my family members suffered at the hands of Nazi invaders in our ancestral towns in Poland and Hungary. My material grandfather, who lived with me and my family, left his family in Krosno, Poland where nine of his siblings, and extended family were all rounded up, marched into the woods, and shot at close range by Nazi soldiers.

To compare events and conditions in the contemporary United States to the Nazi's "final solution" of the Jews amounts not only to historical revisionism to the maximum, but more importantly, it trivializes the extreme conditions under which so many people, Jews and others, suffered from the dehumanization, marginalization, surveillance, arrest, incarceration, torture, "medical" experimentation, rape, murder, and incineration.

So I ask, how many more politicians, pundits, and individuals are going to liken former President Barack Obama to Adolf Hitler and to Joseph Stalin (the two latter who perpetrated opposing political philosophies), and the United States to these forms of government?

I hold both extremes – the Holocaust deniers and the Holocaust revisionists – as offensive to the good people who were all taken from us far too soon. Let them rest in peace. Let the truth prevail.

References

Hypocrisy and Stupidity of Gun Control Advocates on Facebook. Retrieved 9/9/2019, https://www.facebook.com/HaSoGCA.

Chapter Sixteen

Gun Silencers Mute Actual Causes of Gun Violence

Following each high-visibility episode of gun violence in the United States, politicians and other community and national leaders spout their often-repeated worn-out platitudes and false claims regarding the actual causes of this lethal epidemic plaguing the country. Their words all-to-often result in the silencing of the root causes of the problem.

"Sending my best wishes and prayers."

Of course, people of goodwill and compassion express this sentiment to people and communities suffering trauma and grief. This can help to begin the often-long healing process at a time of unfathomable tragedy by providing essential solace to survivors. It also gives those of us who feel powerlessness during these occasions at least a limited sense of standing with others. This expression, though, falls far short of a solution, which morphs into mere platitude when those in positions of power fail to work toward real solutions.

"This is not the time to talk about politics."

After virtually every firearms-related slaughter, a common pattern has emerged: when advocates rightly raise issues of safety regulations, politicians retreat to their deflective tactic of reciting that "now is not the time." Moments pass leading to the next political issue (for example, healthcare or storm disaster relief) pushing gun violence out of the headlines as action is not taken, then the next high-visibility gun massacre blares out, politicians again claim "now is not the time," and the cycle repeats *ad infinitum*.

"It's about better securing our schools."

When politicians make proposals for reducing gun violence, especially in our schools, they suggest such methods as installing metal detectors, self-locking building entrances, constant and updated emergency drills for the entire school population, and training for staff, teachers, and administrators. Increasingly, policy makers advocate adding to the number of armed security monitors, and even arming teachers and administrators as "first-line" defenders.

This latter tactic follows National Rifle Association Executive VP Wayne LaPierre's argument that "The only thing that stops a bad guy with a gun is a good guy with a gun." In fact, the NRA produces stickers and hats inscribed with the motto: "Guns Save Lives." But is this true? Several studies show the opposite.

The lead researcher, Charles Branas et al. (2009), in a University of Pennsylvania study concluded that by arming people as a defensive measure:

> There was an expectation that we should surely find a protective value. [But having a gun] on average was found not to be protective in assaults .... Although successful defensive gun uses can and do occur, the findings of this study do not support the perception that such successes are likely.

In another research study, Harvard School of Public Health's, Hemenway and Miller (2004) found that contrary to many claims, the chances of violence *increased* in homes with a gun. Branas et al, in their study, concurred:

> [T]here is no credible evidence of a deterrent effect of firearms or that a gun in the home reduces the likelihood or severity of injury during an altercation or break-in.

What proponents of this simplistic and disastrous gun-on-gun philosophy fail to realize in their obsession (yes obsession) with the so-called "freedom" to bear arms is that it is *not* only "criminals who kill people." Having augmented numbers of armed school personnel increases the risk for accidental injury and death while offering no guarantees of stopping acts of violence. Fighting fire with fire results in hotter and quicker-moving blazes.

"Guns don't kill people. People kill people."

Actually, people with guns kill people more often and at significantly higher rates than people who don't have guns. Let's take a comparative example.

As stated previously in the Introduction & Overview, before and up to 1996, Australia had relatively high rates of murder, but an incident at Port Arthur, Tasmania, April 28, 1996, was the proverbial straw that broke the poor camel's back. On that date, a man opened fire on a group of tourists killing 35 and wounding another 23. The massacre was the worst mass murder in Australia's history.

Taking decisive action, newly-elected *conservative* Prime Minister, John Howard, negotiated a bipartisan deal between the national, state, and local governments in enacting comprehensive gun safety measures, which included a massive buyback of more than 600,000 semi-automatic rifles and shotguns, and laws prohibiting private fire-arms sales, mandatory registration by owners of all weapons, and the requirement that all potential buyers of guns at the time of purchase give a "genuine reason" other than general or overarching self-defense without documentation of necessity.

By 1996, polls showed overwhelming public support of approximately 90% for the new measures. And though firearms-related injuries and deaths have not totally come to an end, according to the *Christian Science Monitor* (Clark, 2012), homicides by firearms fell by 59% between 1995 and 2006 with *no* corresponding increase in non-firearm-related homicides, and a 65% reduction in gun-related suicides, with no mass shooting within 20 years following implementation of the law.

"It's a mental health issue."

When politicians assert a cause of gun violence, they invariably lay blame on people with mental disabilities. For example, NRA's Wayne LaPierre accused "delusional killers" for the violence, and he called for a "national registry" of all persons diagnosed with mental illness (Berkowitz, 2014). While this is certainly the case in some specific instances, the clear majority of people with this diagnosis do not manifest violence, and specifically, they are not the primary perpetrators of firearms-related injury and death to others. Rather, they are more often the victims of harassment and violence.

Politicians are merely scapegoating an entire group of people rather than acknowledging the real causes. And while these same politicians call for increased support systems for people with mental health issues, Republicans in Congress have voted to reduce supports. On the issue of keeping guns out of the hands of people with emotional and mental health problems, in December 2016, the Obama administration released policy guidelines mandating that people receiving Social Security payments for severe mental illnesses and those found incapable of managing their finances undergo FBI's National Instant Criminal Background Checks if they request to purchase a weapon.

Congress, however, overturned the policy, mostly on party lines (Rifkin, 2017). President Trump signed the measure into law one month after taking office even though following every mass shooting, he referred to these instances as a "mental health problem" as he did again after 17 students and their teachers were recently killed in Parkland, Florida.

In fact, however, reports from the American Psychiatric Association show clearly that mass shootings by people with serious mental illness represent less than 1% of all yearly gun-related homicides (Knoll & Annas, 2017). In addition, research from Columbia and Duke Universities found that "only 3–5% of violent acts are attributable to serious mental illness, and most do not involve guns" (Applebaum & Swanson, 2010).

More recently, a study conducted by the National Council for Mental Wellbeing (2019) found that individuals with a serious mental illness, overall they are responsible for less than 4% of all violent acts committed in the United States. Generally, mass shootings comprised less than two-tenths of 1% of murders between 2000 and 2016.

"Fatherlessness in homes of boys and young men"

Another cause has gained currency on the political right: fatherless homes. Susan L. M. Goldberg of PJMedia, for example, argues:

> Issue number one that no one in the mainstream media or government wants to acknowledge: fatherlessness. Specifically, the impact of fatherlessness on the boys who grew up to become school shooters (Goldberg, 2018).

Goldberg refers to Warren Farrell and John Grey's book *The Boy Crisis* (2018).

> Minimal or no father involvement, whether due to divorce, death, or imprisonment, is common to Adam Lanza, Elliott Rodgers, Dylan Roof and Stephen Paddock .... In the case of 19-year-old Nikolas Cruz, he was adopted at birth. His adoptive dad died when Nikolas was much younger, and doubtless the challenges of this fatherlessness was compounded by the death of his adoptive mom three and a half months ago (Goldberg, 2018).

By implication, the political right is asserting that women-headed households are inferior to those that are male-headed, and, ironically, that a family headed by two fathers in partnership is the best – though they have heartedly disputed this.

Hypermasculinity Combined with Widescale Availability of Firearms

In one year, 2020, gun violence resulted in the homicide of approximately 20,000 people and injury to another nearly 40,000, and in the suicide of approximately 24,000 (Thebault & Rindler, 2021). Murder is primarily a male act in 90% of the cases when the gender of the perpetrator is known. In mass shootings, 98%+ are enacted by males. In 2018, 340 mass shootings were recorded in the United States (Robinson & Gould, 2018). But regulations on firearms challenge the promises of a patriarchal system based on notions of hypermasculinity with the elements taken to the *extreme* of control, domination over others and the environment, competitiveness, autonomy, rugged individualism, strength, toughness, forcefulness, and decisiveness, and, of course, never having to ask for help or assistance. Concepts of cooperation and community responsibility are pushed to the sidelines or often discarded. This connected to the easy legal access to firearms presents a recipe for disaster playing itself out so many times in the United States that is has become routine.

The causes for the plague of gun-related murders holding grip on our nation, nonetheless, is multifaceted and complicated, but not necessarily and only for the reasons articulated on the political right. When they mention causes and solutions, they virtually never bring up the words "guns" or "firearms regulations" other than to discount and reject the cause and effect relationship.

The primary distinction separating the United States from other wealthier highly industrialized countries around world that boast extremely low rates of gun deaths and injuries, in fact, murders overall by any means, is our nations' disastrous positions on guns and the laws meant to regulate them.

Does the United States have so many more cases of mental illness, diagnosed and not? Are schools in the United States significantly "softer targets" than schools, for example, in Australia, Japan, or Sweden? Do boys and young men come from "fatherless" homes at radically higher rates than in these other countries? And why are we not seeing similar violence-prone behaviors in girls and young women from motherless (or fatherless) homes? And why don't people on the right talk more often about what effects the fathers who remain in the home, but who inflict abuse on family members, have on the behaviors of these members?

As with all large-scale social problems, we miss the key causes and solutions when we focus solely on individualized cases instead of viewing the essential systemic issues. The major underlying cause by far for the U.S. having the highest rates of firearms deaths and injuries in Western "democracies" is the unprecedented number of these weapons, their relatively easy accessibility, and the lack of political courage by our elected offices to take decisive action by placing common-sense safety regulations on the sale, use, capacity, velocity, and amount of guns in private ownership.

Contrary to Executive VP of the National Rifle Association, Wayne LaPierre's, often-repeated claim: "To stop a bad guy with a gun, it takes a good guy with a gun," more appropriately and going to the root of the NRA's chokehold on the political process, I say: "To stop a bad legislator with the NRA, it takes a good voter with a ballot!"

Why do politicians and many residents of the U.S. continue to deny, deflect, diffuse, dispose, and dispense with raising issues revolving around the massive and virtually unrestricted availability of firearms, some reaching military-grade capability, as the prime reason for the epidemic of gun violence in the United States? While the answer is detailed, I present a quick and appropriate glance at the problem:

National Rifle Association Campaign Donations, 2016

John McCain (R, AZ) – $7.74 million
Richard Burr (R, NC) – $6.99 million
Roy Blunt (R, MO) – $4.55 million
Thom Tillis (R, NC) – $4.42 million
Cory Gardner (R, CO) – $3.88 million
Marco Rubio (R, FL) – $3.30 million
Joni Ernst (R, IA) – 3,124,273
Rob Portman (R, OH) – $3,061,941
Todd Young (R, IN) – $2.9 million
Bill Cassidy (R, lA) – $2.86 million
French Hill (R, AR) – $1.09 million
Ken Buck (R, CO) – $800,544

David Young (R, IA) – $707,662
Mike Simpson, (R, ID) – $385,731
Greg Gianforte (R, MT) – $344,630
Donald Trump (R) – $21 million

And these are just some of the largest recipients of this blood money.

References

Applebaum, P. S., & Swanson, J. W. (2010, July 1). Law & psychiatry: Gun laws and mental illness: how sensible are the current restrictions? *Psychiatric Services*. Retrieved 9/13/2019, https://ps.psychiatryonline.org/doi/full/10.1176/ps.2010.61.7.652.

Berkowitz, B. (2014, December 17). People with mental illness are scapegoated as cause of mass shootings. *Buzzflash*. Retrieved 9/9/2019, http://legacy.buzzflash.com/commentary/people-with-mental-illnesses-are-scapegoated-as-cause-of-mass-gun-shootings.

Branas, C. C., Richmond, T. S., Culhand, D. P., Ten Have, T. R., & Wiebe, D. J. (2009, November). Investigating the connection between gun possession and gun assault. *American Journal of Public Health, 99*(11), 2034–2040.

Clark, H. (2012, December 24). *Could the U.S. learn from Australia's gun control laws? Christian Science Monitor.* Retrieved 9/13/2019, https://www.csmonitor.com/World/Asia-Pacific/2012/1224/Could-the-US-learn-from-Australia-s-gun-control-laws)

Farrell, W., & Grey, J. (2018). *The boy crisis: Why our boys are struggling and what we can do about it.* Dallas, TX: BenBella Books.

Goldberg, S. L. M. (2018, February 17). When will we have the guts to link fatherlessness to school shootings? PJ Media. Retrieved 9/13/2019, https://pjmedia.com/lifestyle/will-guts-link-fatherlessness-school-shootings/?print=true&singlepage=true.

Hemenway, D., & Miller, M. (2004). Gun threats against and self-defense gun use by California adolescents. *Archives of Pediatrics and Adolescent Medicine, 158*, 395–400.

Knoll, J. L. IV, & Annas, G. D. (2017). *Mass shootings and mental illness.* Washinton, DC: American Psychiatric Association Publishing.

National Council for Mental Wellbeing. (2019). Mass violence in America: Causes, Impacts, and Solutions. Washington, D.C.

Rifkin, J. (2017, March 26). Four Senate Democrats voted for law expanding gun access to those with severe mental illness. *GovTrack Insider*. Retrieved 9/13/2019, https://govtrackinsider.com/four-senate-democrats-voted-for-law-expanding-gun-access-to-those-with-severe-mental-illness-923d3a70fe3.

Robinson, M., & Gould, S. (2018). There were 340 mass shootings in the US in 2018 – here's the full list. *Business Insider*. Retrieved 9/13/2019, https://www.businessinsi der.com/how-many-mass-shootings-in-america-this-year-2018-2.

Thebault, R. & Rindler, D. (2021). Shootings never stopped during the pandemic: 2020 was the deadliest gun violence year in decades. *The Washington Post*, 3/21/2021.

Chapter Seventeen

Firearms Under Congressional Knowledge Undermining Survival

At an impromptu press conference in November 2018, President Donald Trump blamed mental illness as the cause for the attack at a California college bar in the continuing epidemic of gun violence and mass shooting in the country. Speaking to a gaggle of reporters at the White House, Trump described the gunman as "a very sick puppy" who had "a lot of problems."

The suspected shooter, who died at the scene, was a 28-year-old Marine veteran. Though investigators had not yet determined a motive or whether mental illness was a factor, Trump touted his efforts at confronting post-traumatic stress disorder among war veterans. He refused, however, to answer questions on gun control.

"It's [NOT] a mental health issue."

Yes, for someone to take another's life in acts other than self-defense or in war, the perpetrator could most likely be considered not fully mentally healthy. According to Jeffrey Swanson, though, a professor of psychiatry at Duke University,

We have a strong responsibility as researchers who study mental illness to try to debunk that myth. I say as loudly and as strongly and as frequently as I can, that mental illness is *not* a very big part of the problem of gun violence in the United States (Swanson, in Beck, 2016).

Applebaum & Swanson (2010) and other researchers found that in all violence – firearms and other forms – in the United States, only 3–5% is attributable to schizophrenia, bipolar disorder, or depression (the disorders most connected with violence). Most of the violence (approximately 96%) cannot be linked to mental illness.

If we are to lay blame for the violence, we must first point to the firearms manufacturers and lobbyists and their friends in Congress and state legislatures who have perpetrated the condition I call the "Firearms Under Congressional Knowledge Undermining Survival," or FUCK US.

Each person and as a collective nation, we collude and contribute in perpetuating this condition each time we forget merely one day or one week following a tragedy about the innocent victims who were tragically taken from us far too soon.

Each person and as a collective nation, we collude and contribute to this condition each time we fail to speak out to our legislators to enact common-sense firearms control policies.

Each person and as a collective nation, we collude and contribute to this condition each time we think we cannot make a difference in reducing this scourge.

Each person and as a collective nation, we collude and contribute to this condition each time we close down and shut off emotionally to the point of numbness as we witness yet another scene of carnage on our TV screens before reporters turn over coverage to tomorrow's local weather forecast.

As a Jew and member of a family of relatives who suffered Nazi atrocities, I surprised myself by feeling relatively nothing as I learned about the horrific shooting murders from an antisemitic hate crime on October 27, 2018 at the Tree of Life Synagogue in Pittsburgh killing 11 parishioners and wounding 6 others, including four brave police officers.

In the aftermath, I continually watched and read as many reports as I could to stay informed. I learned about the heroic stories of courage and self-sacrifice by police and parishioners alike, and about the selfless commitment by a Jewish nurse in treating the suspected shooter. In the following days, still feeling very little, I learned the poignant and beautiful stories of people who were murdered, including Sylvan, 86, and Bernice Simon, 84, who married at Tree of Life over 60 years ago. And Dr. Jerry Rabinowitz, a primary care physician who treated people with HIV with care and compassion since the earliest outbreak of the pandemic.

Rose Mallinger, who at age 97 was the oldest killed that day, and her daughter Andrea who was injured. In a public statement, Rose's family wrote:

> To Bubbe, family was everything. She knew her children, her grandchildren and her great-grandchild better than they knew themselves. She retained her sharp wit, humor and intelligence until the very last day (Grinberg et al., 2018).

But then my emotions soared from the depths of my being and tears flowed uncontrollably as I heard the stories of Cecil and David Rosenthal, brothers and familiar faces at Tree of Life. They usually arrived first at the synagogue to greet people with friendship and with love as they came for services. Cecil and David were inseparable as constant supports for one another and for parishioners. Early in their lives, physicians diagnosed them as "intellectually" or "developmentally disabled."

But we must question whether the brothers Rosenthal had "disabilities." We must question whether any disability they may have had was imposed upon them by a society that attempted to define them. Was their disability, rather and more profoundly, perpetrated by a society that failed to protect them – and all the precious lives taken by gun violence – from the ultimate of all disabilities: death.

Each person and as a collective nation can cure the condition of Firearms Under Congressional Knowledge Undermining Survival if we are willing to work together to arrive at common-sense solutions to end the scourge that is disabling our nation.

References

Applebaum, P. S., & Swanson, J. W. (2010, July 1). Law & psychiatry: Gun laws and mental illness: how sensible are the current restrictions? *Psychiatric Services*. Retrieved 9/13/2019, https://ps.psychiatryonline.org/doi/full/10.1176/ps.2010.61.7.652.

Beck, J. (2016, June 7). Untangling gun violence from mental illness. *The Atlantic*.

Grinberg, E., McLaughlin, E. C., Sidner, S., & Stapleton, A. (2018, November 1). 11 people were gunned down at a Pittsburgh synagogue. Here are their stories. CNN. Retrieved 9/13/2019, https://www.cnn.com/2018/10/28/us/pittsburgh-synagogue-shooting-victims/index.html.

Chapter Eighteen

The Paradox of Legislation

On November 5, 2017, in Sutherland Springs, Texas, a man in tactical-style gear shot and killed 26 people at the First Baptist Church, including adults, children, and a fetus, and he wounded 20 others.

On May 28, 2018, at Santa Fe High School in Texas, a 17-year-old male student shot and killed ten people – eight students and two teachers – and wounded 13 others.

On August 3, 2019, at Walmart near the Cielo Vista Mall in El Paso, Texas, a white nationalist espousing racist views shot and killed 22 people and wounded 24 others.

On September 1, 2019, a man went on a shooting spree on the highways of West Texas killing seven people and wounding 22 others.

In June 2019, a series of new gun measures passed by the Texas legislature and was signed into law by Republican Governor Greg Abbott taking effect on September 1.

While four of the top 10 deadliest mass shootings since 1949 in the U.S. occurred in the state of Texas, one might speculate that legislators there would tighten regulations on firearms. But contrary to reason and logic, one would be seriously (and deadly) mistaken. In fact, Texans are now saddled with even looser firearms laws, which represent some of the the most lenient in the nation.

One of the new measures further clarifies that it is legal for licensed gun owners to tote their weapons into houses of worship, unless a posted sign announces otherwise. In addition, licensed gun owners, including school employees, may store their weapons and ammunition in locked vehicles on school campuses if these are out in plain view. The law also removes the limit of the number of school marshals who can carry guns on school premises. Landlords can now not forbid their legally gun-owning tenets from keeping weapons and ammunition on the property. And handgun owners may now carry concealed weapons without a license for up to 48 hours when having to evacuate in emergencies, such as hurricanes. Another measure grants foster families permission to store guns and ammunition together to make them more readily obtainable for immediate protection instead of having to store them separately. Huh?

Like our actions in curbing climate change by deregulating environmental protections, we fashion legislation making firearms even more accessible to more people as our response to lowering gun deaths. Like bowing to the interests of fossil fuel, logging, mining, and corporate agribusiness industries, legislators kiss the bloody rings of firearms manufacturers and their lobbyists. Thoughtful and reasonable people know that "it's the guns stupid," but are legislators just too stupid or simply detached from reality to know this? Legislators disconnect the best wishes of their constituents with their own (in)actions.

Paradoxically, most legislators disallow people from carrying guns into government buildings. But if guns are good enough to be brought into houses of worship, and legislators seem to worship firearms, then why are guns not good enough to be brought into legislative houses?

Weeks after Texas's new gun measures went into effect, on September 12, 2019, former El Paso Congressperson, Beto O'Rourke, proclaimed during the third Democratic presidential debate at the University of Houston that he supports taking away certain types of guns from their owners through a mandatory governmental buy-back program: "Hell yes, we're going to take your AR-15, your AK-47! We're not going to allow it to be used against our fellow Americans anymore" (*NBC News*, 2019).

O'Rourke described in gruesome detail the damage caused by bullets from these high intensity firearms in obliterating vital bodily organs. If he had been elected President, there would have been virtually no chance of his following through on his campaign pledge owing to massive opposition in the U.S. Congress and the entrenched overarching culture of firearms in the country. But at the very least, he moved the dialogue though possibly killing his chances of situating himself in the Oval Office and in winning statewide office in Texas.

At the time of his courageous declaration, he was a lone star of Texas!

Reference

NBC News. (2019, September 12). Beto O'Rourke on gun control: 'Hell yes we're going to take your AR-15.' Retrieved 9/14/2019, https://www.nbcnews.com/video/beto-o-rourke-hell-yes-we-re-going-to-take-your-ar-15-68832325641.

Chapter Nineteen

Assault Weapons "Good for Home and Battle"

During a stop on his "America First" pro-Trump rally tour with conspiracy theorist Rep. Marjorie Taylor Greene (R-GA) in Dalton, Georgia on Thursday, May 27, 2021, Rep. Matt Gaetz (R-FL) told an audience of supporters that he believes Americans have "an obligation to use" the Second Amendment, particularly in the fight against so-called "cancel culture" in Silicon Valley. Gaetz also told his audience, "The internet's hall monitors out in Silicon Valley, they think they can suppress us, discourage us ... Well, you know what? Silicon Valley can't cancel this movement. Or this rally. Or this congressman." And, finally, Gaetz blared out and laid bare the long held open secret that right-wing gun advocates have contended as the prime reason the founders included the Second Amendment in the U.S. Constitution:

"The Second Amendment is not about, it's not about hunting, it's not about recreation, it's not about sports," Gaetz admitted. "The Second Amendment is about maintaining within the citizenry the ability to maintain an armed rebellion against the government if that becomes necessary. I hope it never does, but it sure is important to recognize the founding principles of this nation and to make sure that they are fully understood."

As the anti-choice coat hanger patriarchal Christian white supremacist warriors hung nooses and spread feces on Capitol grounds on their mission of destruction rummaging around to lynch Vice President Pence and overturn a valid and official election on January 6, 2021, these same "warriors" and millions of others like them fight violently to sanctify their "reading" of the Second Amendment.

They do this while simultaneously fighting every day to deny other people their voter rights, civil rights, LGBTQ rights, women's rights, rights to a fair and impartial judicial process, immigrant rights, freedom of and from religion, the Constitutional balance of power, and, in particular, we the people's rights to safety from firearms. In Gaetz's case, he seemed to have attempted to divert attention away from impending criminal indictments against himself of sex trafficking with underaged girls.

Only two weeks following Goetz interpretation of the Second Amendment, a federal judge in San Diego, California seemed to concur by overturning a 32-year ban of that state's assault style weapons as a "failed experiment" that violates constitutional guarantees to bear arms. U.S. District Judge Roger Benitez, appointed by President George W. Bush, ruled that the state of California, by making these military-style weapons illegal, deprives responsible gun owners of firearms routinely permitted in other states. Benitez handed down his ruling even though the federal government imposed a similar ban for a period of 10 years initiated during the Bill Clinton administration, which was never struck down as "unconstitutional" by the Supreme Court.

The Public Safety and Recreational Firearms Use Protection Act, or the Federal Assault Weapons Ban, a subsection of the Violent Crime Control and Law Enforcement Act of 1994, prohibited the manufacture of certain semi-automatic firearms, defined as assault weapons, and some types of ammunition and "large capacity" magazines for civilian use. The law expired in 2004 in accordance with the law's "sunset provision." It was not reauthorized.

California District Court Judge Benitez, however, saw no problem with semi-automatic assault weapons:

"This case is not about extraordinary weapons lying at the outer limits of Second Amendment protection," he argued. "The banned 'assault weapons' are not bazookas, howitzers, or machine guns. Those arms are dangerous and solely useful for military purposes," his ruling emphasized. "Instead, the firearms deemed 'assault weapons' are fairly ordinary, popular, modern."

Crack cocaine and so-call "designer" drugs are also "fairly ordinary, popular, and modern," but does this make them safe and appropriate for largescale sale?

Benitez went on to state in his ruling:

"Like the Swiss Army knife," he contended, "the popular AR-15 rifle is a perfect combination of home defense weapon and homeland defense equipment. Good for both home and battle."

So, "like the Swiss Army knife," one can take their AR-15 on a lunch outing in the woods to uncork a lovely bottle of French wine or clean one's fingernails after an afternoon of planting petunias in the garden. And what about cutting red construction paper to fashion a brilliant large heart for one's valentine?

Just think about the possibilities of how this is good for both home and battle next time one wishes the kill the Vice President or even the President and the entire Congress each time one's candidate's election was "stolen," or each time Jews deploy their space lasers to burn down rich forested lands, or when Satan-praying pedophiles eat children in one's town, or when Silicon Valley tech companies deprive one of their precious social media platforms.

One can also go into battle by traveling to Italy to take out the people who created and activated Italian military satellites that forced U.S. voting machines to switch Trump votes to Biden's column.

Indeed, "good for both home and battle." But Benitez's ruling is on hold pending appeals.

Chapter Twenty

Gun Safety Reform and "Interest Convergence"

Since a total of 31 people were ruthlessly murdered in gun violence in two separate incidents within hours of each other in El Paso, Texas and Dayton, Ohio in 2019, the civil rights organization, Amnesty International, issued a travel warning to visitors considering journeying to the U.S. among "high levels of gun violence," which the group referred to as a human rights crisis (Amnesty International, 2019). With growing incidents of domestic-grown terrorism perpetrated by avowed Christian white nationalists in the country, the advisory added:

> Depending on the traveler's gender identity, race, country of origin, ethnic background, or sexual orientation, they may be at higher risk of being targeted with gun violence, and should plan accordingly.

Several countries have issued their own warnings to travelers coming to the U.S. including Uruguay, Venezuela, Japan, France, Germany, Netherlands, Ireland, Canada and New Zealand.

In a statement issued by Japan's Minister of Foreign Affairs, the diplomatic mission warned Japanese citizens to "be aware of the potential for gunfire incidents everywhere in the United States," and referred to the country as a "gun society" (Sugiyama, 2019). The foreign ministry of Uruguay (Rodrigo, 2019) warned its residents to apply caution "against growing indiscriminate violence, mostly for hate crimes" fueled by racism and discrimination, "which cost more than 250 people their lives in the first seven months of this year." The advisory also warned Uruguayan residents traveling to the country "to avoid areas with large concentrations of people like theme parks, shopping centers, art festivals, religious events, food festivals and any kind of cultural or sporting gathering," noting the "indiscriminate possession of firearms by the population."

The German government's travel warning to the U.S. refers to the "easy" access and possession of firearms and warns of the relatively common shootings throughout the country (Auswärtiges Amt, 2019). The French diplomatic service alerted French visitors that "carrying firearms is authorized and common" in several U.S. states. "Visitors must therefore, in all circumstances, keep their calm and sang-froid (cold blood)."

"Travelers to the United States should remain cautious that the country does not adequately protect people's right to be safe, regardless of who they might be," stated Ernest Coverson, campaign manager for the End Gun Violence Campaign at Amnesty International U.S.A. (Amnesty International, 2019) and added.

> People in the United States cannot reasonably expect to be free from harm – a guarantee of not being shot is impossible. Once again, it is chillingly clear that the U.S. government is unwilling to ensure protection against gun violence.

The continuing and ever-increasing scourge of gun violence has placed the United States under an international spotlight. Its then president, Donald Trump, spoke with typical bravado and threatened other countries issuing travel advisories. "If they did that, we'd just reciprocate," Trump said at an impromptu interview with reporters. "We are a very reciprocal nation with me as the head," he continued. "When somebody does something negative to us in terms of a country, we do it to them" (Jackson, 2019). This President seemed not to care how the United States was regarded around the world with his highly touted

"America First" policy, which resulted in "America Alone" on many policy issues.

Our standing and leadership position in the world, however, depends on how closely we are perceived to uphold our expressed values of protecting human dignity and human rights, of serving as a safe and supportive place for people to live and visit, and to uphold the doctrine that all people are created equal.

Following each tragic episode of gun violence, we hear politicians mouth words of possible solutions, but after the news turns to other issues, the sounds of silence engulf the airwaves where proposals once reverberated.

How much longer will legislators, primarily on the Republican side of the aisle, hibernate within the pockets of the gun lobbies and manufacturers before they care more about saving lives and restoring the diminished image of the U.S. before they come "right" to the side of history rather than to politics? To remain viable, the GOP must craft a diversity of thought and a diversity of policies to give people something to vote for, something to embrace, something that makes people's lives better, rather than rehashing the policies of the past. They must let go of the policies of fear, hate, and division not only on issues of immigration but also related to real gun safety measures.

The late Dr. Derrick Bell of New York University Law School forwarded the theory of "interest convergence" (Bell, 1973), meaning that white people will support racial justice only when they understand and see that there is something in it for them, when there is a "convergence" between the interests of white people and racial justice.

Bell asserted that the Supreme Court ended the longstanding policy in 1954 of "separate but equal" in *Brown v. Board of Education* because it presented to the world, and in particular, to the Soviet Union during the height of the Cold War, a United States that supported civil and human rights as the USSR exposed the extreme racial tensions in its propaganda campaigns.

Let us take another example: The Church of Latter-Day Saints (LDS) president, Brigham Young, instituted a policy on February 13, 1849, emanating from "divine revelation" and continuing until as recently as 1978 forbidding ordination of black men of African descent from the ranks of LDS priesthood. This policy prohibited black men and women from participating in the Temple Endowment and Sealing, which the Church requires for the highest degree of salvation. The policy likewise restricted black people from attending or participating in temple marriages.

Young attributed this restriction to the sin of Cain, Adam and Eve's eldest son, who killed his brother Abel: "What chance is there for the redemption of the Negro?" stated Young in 1849 following declaration of his restrictive policy. "The Lord had cursed Cain's seed with blackness and prohibited them the Priesthood" (FairMormon, n.d.).

The twelfth LDS Church president, Spencer W. Kimball, who served from 1973 to his death in 1985, was supposedly touched with a vision, and he reversed the ban, referring to it as "the long-promised day." Well, we can ask today whether "revelation" or interest conversion was the determining factor in granting black people full membership rights in the Church at a time of ongoing and heightened civil rights activities in the United States and an increase in LDS missionary recruitment efforts throughout the African continent.

Possibly when the Republican Party realizes its interests to follow the expressed wishes of the majority of the electorate, maybe then the GOP will join with many of the Democrats to craft and pass comprehensive and compassionate gun safety reforms and immigration reforms, and stop the politics of division toward people of color, LGBTQ people, Muslims, and all people who do not identify as Christian. Maybe then and only then will the Republican Party abandon policies that embolden Christian white nationalists, which may save the Party from itself.

References

Amnesty International. (2019). Travel advisory: United States of America. Retrieved 9/14/2019, https://www.amnestyusa.org/our-work/government-relations/advocacy/travel-advisory-united-states-of-america/.

Auswärtiges Amt (Ministry of Foreign Affairs). (2019, August 14). USA/Vereinigte Staaten: Reise- und Sicherheitshinweise (USA/United States: Safety and travel information). Retrieved 9/14/2019, https://www.auswaertiges-amt.de/de/aussenpolitik/laender/usa-node/usavereinigtestaatensicherheit/201382.

Bell, D. (1973). *Race, racism, and American law.* New York: Aspen Publishers.

FairMormon. (n.d.). Mormonism and the "curse of Cain." Retrieved 9/14/2019, https://www.fairmormon.org/answers/Mormonism_and_racial_issues/Blacks_and_the_priesthood/The_%22curse_of_Cain%22_and_%22curse_of_Ham%22.

Jackson, D. (2019, August 9). Trump threatens to retaliate against countries like Japan, Uruguay that issued travel warnings. *USA Today.* Retrieved 9/14/2019, https://www.usatoday.com/story/news/politics/2019/08/09/trump-threatens-retaliation-over-travel-warnings-against-us/1965898001/.

Rodrigo, C. M. (2019, August 5). Uruguay issues travel alert for US, warning of deadly hate crimes. *The Hill.* Retrieved 9/14/2019, https://thehill.com/latino/456251-uruguay-issues-travel-alert-for-us-warning-of-deadly-hate-crimes.

Chapter Twenty-One

A Day in the Life of a Narcissist on the Twittersphere

February 14, 2018 (Valentine's Day) began like any typical day for the community in and around Marjory Stoneman Douglas High School in Parkland, Florida: parents said good bye as students left for school, faculty and students met for classes, administrators and staff were on hand to maintain operations working to meet the diverse needs of all involved. But soon before the end of the school day, a disgruntled and apparently deranged former student entered the high school with an AR-15 military-style weapon, which he legally purchased, and randomly fired at anyone in his field of vision. When he had completed his evil task, 17 innocent precious lives had been extinguished with another 15 injured, some critically. Though the duty of Consoler-In-Chief is not inscribed into the job description of the President of the United States, in times of national and local tragedies, our past Presidents have been thrust into the role with differing degrees of effectiveness.

Following the deadly and destructive attack by the Japanese on Pearl Harbor on December 7, 1941, President Franklin D. Roosevelt spoke to the nation with a firm and confident resolve promising the country that his administration would take appropriate steps to right the wrongs perpetrated upon us, and by so doing, assured a frightened and enraged nation that the government was working in the people's best interests.

President George W. Bush brought a devastated nation together as he stood with first responders on heaps of rubble that only several hours earlier had been the mighty World Trade Center Towers, after numerous vicious strikes along the east coast on September 11, 2001.

Presidents Bill Clinton and Barack Obama presented the right tone of compassion and empathy following the increasing number of high-visibility mass shooting episodes plaguing our nation. The ordinarily cool "no drama Obama" wiped away a tear and exposed his frustration over the easy accessibility of high-powered rifles following the dev-asting murder of 20 precious babies and their teachers at Sandy Hook Elementary School on December 14, 2012. And he led all assembled in singing "Amazing Grace" in memory of the nine lives snuffed out by an avowed Christian white supremacist at the historic Emanuel African Methodist Episcopal Church in Charleston, South Carolina on June 17, 2015.

The best one could say about Donald Trump in stepping into this role, however, was that he seemed completely incapable of getting out of his own way, and he lacked the compassion, empathy, and sense of proper decorum to offer aid and comfort in times of tragedy and grief.

One day following the murders at Marjory Stoneman Douglas High School, Trump appeared on camera reading prepared remarks, which he unlikely personally wrote. Lacking emotion of any sort, his comments rang false. For one who has demonstrated no faith in any power outside himself, he talked about "praying for the victims and their families." As the most divisive president in modern history, it was almost laughable when he uttered: "We are all joined together as one American family, and your suffering is our burden also."

He continued that there are people "who will do anything at all" to keep young people safe, but he, apparently, did not position himself among those willing to "do anything at all" since he advised young peo-ple to rely on teachers, family, police and faith leaders. And as someone who possessed the authority to help resolve the scourge of gun violence in the U.S., he never once mentioned the root of the problem: guns, since he and his Republican coconspirators are beholden to the National Rifle Association, firearms manufacturers, and their blood money.

Trump then made a brief excursion from his luxury resort at Mar-a-Lago to the Florida hospital serving the needs of remaining injured survivors of the tragic shooting. He stayed long enough for a few photo ops, and departed for his resort where he engaged in a joyous disco party. While at the hospital, I half-expected him to toss wrappers of tissues to the injured, so they could wipe away tears for themselves and their lost companions, as he had insensitively thrown rolls of paper towels to the victims of the Puerto Rican devastation after a powerful hurricane in September 2017.

That night, however, in an apparent cheese-burger-intoxicated stupor, this Sociopath-In-Chief once again made other people's pain and tragedy about himself. He posted in a Tweet:

> Very sad that the FBI missed all of the many signals sent out by the Florida school shooter. This is not acceptable. They are spending too much time trying to prove Russian collusion with the Trump campaign - there is no collusion. Get back to the basics and make us all proud!
>
> 11:08 PM – Feb 17, 2018

If that were not base (in all senses of the word) enough, he followed with a Tweet connecting violence in Florida with the contentious issue of immigration reform:

> Just like they don't want to solve the DACA problem [Deferred Action for Childhood Arrivals – DREAMers], why didn't the Democrats pass gun control legislation when they had both the House & Senate during the Obama Administration. Because they didn't want to, and now they just talk!
>
> 6:45 PM – Feb 17, 2018

These utterances fell lower than Trump's typical narcissistic egotistic insensitivity all the way to the lowest depths of unfitness to serve in the most powerful position in the world. Along with so many other instances, this again proved that Donald Trump had little to no ability to care about or for others, and even less about the overarching interests of this country. He did not care whether foreign nations committed cyberwar upon our democratic institutions. He did not care about the work and commitment of members of his own justice department.

Trump seemed to forget that he reignited the issue of DACA by decertifying the program. And while Donald seemingly could not chew gum and walk at the same time, he did not understand that literally tens-of-thousands of people work at the FBI, and that they are capable of investigating the misdeeds of the Russian government while looking into domestic terrorism.

Did the FBI fail in its examination of the shooter in Parkland, Florida before his deadly rampage? Most certainly! Could it have done better? Most certainly! Must they be held accountable? Yes! Is the FBI to blame for the epidemic of gun-related violence in schools and in the larger society? Absolutely not! That charge lays on the steps of our legislative houses, firearms manufacturers, sellers, and political lobbyists such as the National Rifle Association.

Throughout the day following Trump's visit at the hospital, he Tweeted numerous times about the Justice Department's investigation of Russian hacking, and on each occasion he either again declared his total innocence, or proclaimed his exhortation, even before final conclusions had been reached by prosecutors. Virtually the only message of hope and healing to come from the Trump family was a Tweet by the First Lady, Melania on her official FLOTUS account:

> I encourage everyone to test the power of kindness on #RandomActs ofKindnessDay. It's an opportunity to teach our children the importance of taking care of one another.
>
> 11:42 AM – Feb 17, 2018

Chapter Twenty-Two

Firearms Debate: A View from Hoplophiliaville

Dr. Sigmund Freud, in his *New Introductory Lectures on Psychoanalysis* (1933), expanded his theories on the interpretations of dreams to include weaponry as symbolizing the genitalia, and in particular, the penis. According to Freud:

> All complicated machines and appliances are very probably the genitals – as a rule the male genitals – in the description of which the symbolism of dreams is as indefatigable as human wit. It is quite unmistakable that all weapons and tools are used as symbols for the male organ: e.g., ploughshare, hammer, gun, revolver, dagger, sword, etc. (Freud, 1908, n.p.).

Along with this, Freud developed his theory of "penis envy" in girls and women. Seeing the father, who has a penis, as the seat of power and authority in the home, stated Freud: "Girls hold their mother responsible for their lack of a penis and do not forgive her for their being thus put at a disadvantage" (Clark, 2019).

While his theories, especially those relating to females, may seem misguided and misogynistic to many of us now, to Freud, the compulsion to own firearms stems from an unconscious need to compensate for a deep-seated psychological sense of insecurity and inadequacy in terms of power: in males, specifically for having a small or smaller-than-desired penis, and in females, in an attempt to symbolically grow a large penis.

In literature among other fields, this is a common trope. For example, in the stage play, Hedda Gabler, by Norwegian playwright, Henrik Ibsen (1890), the play's protagonist possesses a pair of dueling pistols formerly owned by her father. Though Hedda marries a man named George Tesman, she holds onto her family name of Gabler. In the Victorian age, guns were seen as masculine objects, and in Freud's theories, guns symbolized the penis. In this sense, the pistols serve as a continual reminder that she will always be a Gabler like her father, and could likewise indicate that she desires to be a man or even sees herself as a powerful man.

So, was it mere coincidence or, rather, irony, that the Milton Bradley Company of Springfield, Massachusetts, billing itself as the "Maker of the World's Best Games," introduced a toy for pre- and early-teen boys in the closing years of World War I: its "Big Dick" machine gun? In its 1918 print ad circulating in various publicans aimed (no pun intended) at young boys, above a drawing of the product ejecting what appeared as wooden pellets, in large serif bold lettering and as if coming from the loud commands of a military officer: "Ready! Aim! FIRE!" And then below: " 'Big Dick' " "American Boys Attention" followed by smaller lettering: "Get at the breech of a Big Dick! Exciting fun; No danger. Shoots thirty-six (36) wooden bullets as fast as you can turn the firing-crank."

Inside a rectangular box, the makers provide the product's dimensions: "24 inches long, 9 inches high, 36 shots a minute." And if this does not convince boys to pester their parents to run to the toy shore to purchase the gun, the ad makes one last justification: "Big Dick is modeled after the machine guns used on the European battlefronts and for indoor war play has no equal."

Did people at the time use the word "Dick" as a substitute for "penis"? And more importantly, how can this "toy" pose no danger to another's eyes or other areas of the body upon contact? Why does the ad specifically target boys and not girls? What messages does this product send regarding the socialization of young males and gender roles, about the place of firearms in our society, and about the supposed glory and heroism of war at the beginning of the deadliest war-prone century in human history (*man*-kind)?

In their effort to counter this societal discourse often circulated by opponents of the sweeping and ingrained firearms culture embedded in the fabric of the United States, many gun rights advocates, members of what I have termed the "Pro-Firearms with No More Regulations Movement," have attempted to turn the psychological tables by attaching themselves to an alleged statement Sigmund Freud supposedly made: "A fear of weapons is a sign of retarded sexual and emotional maturity."

The problem for members of this movement, however, is that Freud *never* uttered this. Neither this statement nor anything even approaching it appears in any of Freud's works in any of its translations. It is, rather, a quote falsely attributed to Freud, an opinion now circulating around the internet of Freud's theories, specifically his 10th Lecture, "Symbolism in Dreams," in *General Introduction to Psychoanalysis* (1900).

Be that as it may, members of this Pro-Firearms with No More Regulations Movement have embraced a new term – stemming from the (non-) quote attributed to Sigmund Freud – in their attempts to make themselves come across as rational while pathologizing those of us who are working for common sense gun control.

Though the term holds no official acceptance within any medical or psychological academy or association, and the American Psychiatric Association has not included it anywhere within the most recent or previous versions of its *Diagnostic and Statistical Manual of Mental Disorders* (DSM), an American marine, Jeff Cooper, in 1962 coined the term "hoplophobia" (from the Greek ὅπλον - *hoplon*, meaning "arms" or "weapons," and φόβος – *phobos*, meaning "fear") to explain a so-called irrational aversion to weapons, or the fear of firearms or of armed citizens.

These hoplophile members of the Pro-Firearms with No More Regulations Movement may actually believe this strategy holds promise in silencing us, and help them to counter the psychological discourse connected to their obsessive attachments to firearms, but it will fail ("hoplophile" – from the Greek ὅπλον - *hoplon*, meaning "arms" or "weapons," and ὅπλον - *philia*, meaning "love" or "intense friendship or sexual desire for").

Most clear-thinking people understand that "hoplophobia" itself is an *irrational* term since there is nothing "irrational" about fearing that one could be listed among the 11,000+ gun-related homicides each year in the U.S., many perpetrated by people who purchased firearms *legally*. There is nothing "irrational" about fearing for women or men who date or are married to men with anger management issues who legally purchased firearms. There is nothing irrational about fearing for the safety of children who reside in homes with firearms.

To paraphrase something else Freud *never* said or wrote, "Sometimes a cigar is just a cigar" (sorry to expose yet another folk myth), I say simply, "Fear of guns is just fear of guns since we have very good reason to fear guns. They kill, maim, permanently disable, and unalterably and negatively change lives."

As a society, we must decide whether we will continue doing things over and over again as we have in the past and expecting different results (definition of "insanity" often attributed to Albert Einstein), or try something new for our country in an attempt to extricate ourselves from the blood bath we ourselves created.

References

Clark, J. (2019). 'Pregnant People?', *Colombia Law Review Online, 19*(6). n.p.

Freud, S. (1933). *New introductory lectures on psychoanalysis*. London, UK: Hogarth Press.

Freud, S. (1908, December). On the sexual theories of children. *Sexual-Probleme, 4*(12), 763–779.

Freud, S. (1900). Symbolism in dreams. In S. Freud & J. Riviere (Eds.), *General Introduction to Psychoanalysis*. Garden City, NY: Garden City Pub. Co. [©1943].

Ibsen, H. (1890). *Hedda Gabler*. London, UK: William Heinemann.

Chapter Twenty-Three

Patriarchy, Toxic Hypermasculinity, & Firearms

Look at that. A pillow biting chicken queen, who sidelines as an attention whore. Obsessed with his lack of masculinity, and still trying to work out his rage because mommy and daddy didn't accept him. Sees guns as a symbol of the masculinity he could never achieve, so he hates them, and the people connected with them ….

This quote by the administrator of the Disarmanuts Facebook page in response to one of my gun safety commentaries exposes a clear example of something the media rarely underscore in our current culture of gun violence: the gendered character of that violence.

With the thousands of individual and mass shootings of four or more victims in the United States each year, men, mostly white men (Chemaly, 2016) committed the overwhelming majority. Since 2013, hundreds of school shooting have occurred effecting hundreds of thousands of students and school personnel (Everytown, 2019). We have also seen numerous incidents of gun violence executed at family health clinics, houses of worship, community centers, and other sites with a disproportionate number of female employees. The Pew Research Center found that white men own over 60% of the gun in the U.S. Overall, 74% of gun owners are male and 82% are white (Flock, 2013).

It is no mere coincidence that generally women (69%) favor stricter gun control regulations more than men (47%) (Pew Research Center, 2017). According to a Quinnipiac University poll of registered voters, 71% of women supported a nationwide ban on assault weapons compared with 46% of men (AEI, 2016). The Gallop organization found that men (56%) feel safer with a gun in the home than do women (39%), since women are by far the largest group of victims of domestic violence (Casper, 2013).

In my attempt to come to an understanding why so many people oppose and resist common sense firearms safety regulations, I have developed a proposition that regulations on firearms challenge the promises of a patriarchal system based on notions of hypermasculinity with the elements taken to the *extreme* of control: domination over others and the environment, competitiveness, autonomy, rugged individualism, strength, toughness, forcefulness, and decisiveness, and, of course, never having to ask for help or assistance. Concepts of cooperation and community responsibility are pushed to the sidelines and discarded.

To test out my theory, I distributed to several Facebook pages my understanding for the reasons why the United States remains among the last of the wealthier Western countries to resist instituting meaningful and appropriate firearms safety measures. Coming from the vast majority of sites devoted to enhancing firearms safety, members responded very positively, as if what I proposed was obvious, as common sense, and as indisputable. Examples of comments I received from these sites included: "Spot on analysis," "Brilliant!," "You said something I have been thinking for years, but you articulated it so well," "Thank you for your clarity," as well as providing some alternative explanations such as: "Follow the Money. Straight to the NRA from Colt, Remington and Smith & Wesson. It is NOT really about the 2nd Amendment for a 'well-regulated militia'; it is about selling weapons to the market of frightened people."

I also reached out to other locations where I was less likely of receiving nearly universal support. Among the sites I contacted included members of a pro-firearms anti-regulations Facebook page calling itself Hypocrisy and Stupidity of Gun Control Advocates. By the site's title alone, I should have been more prepared for the veracity of responses I received.

Demographics and Methodology

Following my initial statements on this Facebook page, approximately 120 or so different people responded. From what I could perceive of their genders or gender identities, no one identified as transgender, while only three identified as female. I could not determine the "racial" identities of the respondents since members did not identify in racial terms.

After I downloaded all of the comments, I coded all responses to identify any emerging themes. To my disappointment, but unfortunately not of much surprise, only 4 or 5 of the total number of responders made some form of reasoned or informed points, from wanting to protect their families to, for the women responders, warding off potential rapists. In addition, two made attempts at standing up to restrain the vast majority who responded out of rage and attack. While the upstanders efforts did not prove effective, at least they tried.

For the remainder of the members who posted during this time, rather than discussing or debating, they spewed venomous attacks in the form of name calling, character assassinations, and direct threats. I report the forms it took. I have kept the language exactly as responders delivered it. I also discuss some of the memes they posted according to the themes that emerged.

Calling My Masculinity into Question

Most members tapped into the larger societal hierarchy of masculinity in terms of the binary of the "Alpha Male" literally and figuratively on top versus the "Beta Male" on the bottom. According to the definitions on Urban Dictionary: "Alpha Male": "1. The leader of the pack/herd/ etc. 2. The dominant male, 3. The main source of population."

I also found the definition of "Alpha Male Syndrome," which I surmise most members on the Facebook site would not embrace, since it is a "psychological ailment when a guy always has to push or boss others around, start fights, talk shit, makes himself the center of attention, assume responsibility for anyone else's triumph while also pushing the blame for his fuck-ups onto others."

And "Beta Male": "an unremarkable, careful man who avoids risk and confrontation. Beta males lack the physical presence, charisma, and confidence of the Alpha male."

All responses associated with this hierarchy referred to me as "Beta" for the purpose of dismissing anything I have to say. I include only a few representative examples:

- "He's a beta male = no relevance."
- "That's some beta male nonsense right there."
- "If ever there were a poster boy for beta male ... " followed by my Facebook picture with my three dogs:

Photo 1: Myself and my three dogs: l-r, Matza, Hamsa, & Nikos.

- In response to my initial posting: "Translation: Yada-yada, buzzword, buzzword, buzzword city, beta male cuckholdry, whining, hail Karl Marx, more yadas and finish off with a death to America."

Photo 2: Myself and my three dogs: l-r, Matza, Hamsa, & Nikos.

Defense of Hypermasculinity

- "... every one of those [elements of hyper-masculinity that Blumenfeld listed on his initial posting] can be attributed to natural human nature. Take that away, and we'd all be a bunch a limp wristed pussies."

Heterosexism & Cissexism

Again, for the purpose of dismissing me, they referred in negative terms to my sexual identity or my gender expression, which they could easily determine by accessing my Facebook page or by initiating a google search. (They could not fathom my identity as "agender" to which they never acknowledged or referred.)

- "The only thing missing from his comment is a cute, transparent rainbow over his profile pic."
- "Fgt" [Faggot]

- "A very learned, articulate, self flagellating fag. Good riddance." [This posting represents the only complement to my intelligence.]
- "Man this oke right here sounds like he went to a Re-Education Camp. I hope they didn't cut your balls off Boet."

Feminization/Sexism

One of the most exploited ways of degrading males within our overarching patriarchal sexist society is to feminize or demasculinize males. This exposes our society's blatant and covert forms of misogyny.

- "Warren …. Aren't you late for your bikini wax?"
- "Another liberal dipshit trying to pussify the American male. Go be a hipster somewhere else."
- "This moron needs to go back to Star Bucks, sip his Latte, and shut his fucking douchey mouth. What a mouth breathing dick bag … Seriously … "
- "Another 'I'm smarter and more enlightened then you' liberal douchebag, who's nowhere near as original as he believes he is. Fuck outta here with that shit."
- "Wtf [What the fuck] are you people smoking?! I'm an INDIVIDUAL. That's not negotiable. Shove this leftist/globalist community bullshit back in whatever orifice you dug it out of. Pansy ass apologists are the reason this Country faces destruction from within."

Many of the respondents' comments linked feminization and what I had thought was the extinct concept of the "hippy." Also, I see that going to "Star Bucks" or "Starbucks" also is feminizing.

- "Trying to drop hippy buzzwords like patriarchal and transabled and overly masculin (*sic*) or masculinization or whatever the fuck else is hip right now. Piss off hippy, I discredit you when you when you do this. It truly does make you a regurgibot. That is a robot that regurgitates the bullshit you soak up in the liberal robot factory/marxist indoctrination system such as liberal biased media driven sensationalist clown colleges across North America. Go piss up a rope and let the adults talk you tight pants scarf combo wearing Starbucks loving social experiment."

Ableism

- "Translation: I throw out big words to sound intellectual when I'm actually a fucking retard who is beyond help."

Protection against Alien Cultures (Racism)

- Individualls (*sic*) are what built this society. The blending of individuals led to the culture. Now alien cultures are expecting to stay segregated, not become American. They are dangerous to the stability of our nation. It's the individual gun owner, under every blade of grass that kept us from being invaded already. This whole topic is exhausting. The ignorance of the intelligent is stupefyingly.

Dehumanization

I have learned many lessons in my studies of genocides perpetrated throughout the ages. Strong leaders whip up sentiments by employing dehumanizing terminology and images while stereotyping and scapegoating entire groups, while other citizens or entire nations look on, often refusing to intervene. Everyone, not only the direct perpetrators of oppression, plays a vital role in the genocides. On a micro level, this is also apparent, for example, in episodes of schoolyard, community-based, as well as electronic forms of bullying.

Several respondents represented me in dehumanizing terms. Some represented me as a dog, or attacked my dogs to attack me:

- "Dude looks like he rubs peanut butter on him so his dogs can lick it off."
- "What did those poor dogs to desreve (*sic*) a complete a idiot?"

- "You see dogs, I see snake food."
- "What dogs? You mean those wussified rats?"

One member literally converted me into a dog using Photoshop to place one of my dog's heads on my shoulders and my head on one of my dog's shoulders. Many referred to me as a "sheep," while others distanced themselves from being placed in this category of "sheep":

- "You've strung a bunch of intelligent sounding words together in an attempt to portray yourself as a learned individual, but have merely come across as a pseudo-intellectual sheep."
- "I'm not a sheep, so no I'm not standing for anymore gun control."

If members do not consider themselves as "sheep" as they "accuse" me, I wonder whether they envision themselves more as wolves or as sheepdogs? I ask this after seeing the film, "American Sniper," in which the protagonist, Chris Kyle (played by Bradley Cooper) remembered something he learned from his father (played by Ben Reed) when he was young. Wayne Kyle: [to his two sons]:

There are three types of people in this world: sheep, wolves, and sheepdogs. Some people prefer to believe that evil doesn't exist in the world, and if it ever darkened their doorstep, they wouldn't know how to protect themselves. Those are the sheep.

Then you've got predators who use violence to prey on the weak. They're the wolves.

And then there are those blessed with the gift of aggression, an overpowering need to protect the flock. These men are the rare breed who live to confront the wolf. They are the sheepdog.

I assume the majority of members on this Facebook page see themselves as "sheepdogs" as protectors of us flock of sheep. What I experienced, however, was a pack of wolves.

Threat of Violence

One of Suzanne Pharr's (1997) common elements of oppression centers on the threat and use of violence by dominant groups who have defined and imposed the social norms upon those who do not or will not conform to these norms. In addition, Iris Marion Young (2004) lists "violence" as one of her five "faces" in her taxonomy looking at the common factors involved in privilege and oppression.

- "Warren J. Blumenfeld do the world a favor and go chug some bleach"
- "Die. Just die. Today. Fucking Liberals."
- "Just yell 'fuck the a.i.d.s. straight into that little pin dick of yours'. Followed by 'since I was diagnosed its been forever since I've had a good fucking' ".

Analysis

Our society promotes what most of us have been very consciously and carefully taught throughout our lives. Gender roles (sometimes called sex roles) include the set of socially-defined roles and behaviors assigned to the sex we are assigned at birth. This can and does vary from culture to culture. Our society recognizes basically two distinct gender roles. One is the "masculine," having the qualities and characteristics attributed to males. The other is the "feminine," having the qualities and characteristics attributed to females. A third gender role, rarely condoned in our society, at least for those assigned "male" at birth, is "androgyny" combining assumed male (*andro*) and female (*gyne*) qualities. A fairly simple way to remember the differences between "sex" and "gender roles" is to consider "sex" as a noun and "gender roles" as a verb (a repeated action).

This all conjures up images of the Hollywood movie "The Truman Show" starring Jim Carrey in the lead role as Truman Burbank. The film documents a man who for most of his life remains unaware that he lives within a human-made artificial set of a reality television show, broadcast 24 hours a day to billions of people around the world. The show's executive producer and director, Christof, placed Truman at birth in the fictitious town of Seahaven, and manipulates every aspect of his life. (I will leave it up to you to analyze why the director of this farce has been given the name "Christof.")

To dissuade Truman from exploring past the limits of the constructed set, Christof pretends to kill Truman's father in a fabricated storm to teach him to fear the water. In addition, actors playing the part of TV news reporters warn of the dangers of travel, and promote the benefits of staying home. However, stemming from some unforeseen glitches in the scenery and unexplained and habitual coincidences in the placement of the actors around him, Truman becomes suspicions until he discovers the truth about the artificiality, manipulation, and control Christof has perpetrated on him for the past 30 years. Truman eventually outwits Christof and escapes the fabricated set into the warmth and brightness of a true sun, and the coolness and wetness of natural rain.

The respondents to my firearms commentaries serve as the director in the larger coercive societal battalions bent on destroying all signs of gender transgressions in young and old alike, and in the maintenance of gender scripts. Most of us function as conscious and unconscious co-directors in this drama each time we enforce gender-role conformity in others, and each time we relegate our critical consciousness by failing to rewrite or destroy the scripts in ways that operate integrally to us. Those who bully, like these respondents, often fulfill the social "function" of establishing and reinforcing the socially constructed scripts handed to them when they entered the play of life. However, each time any of us rewrite the scripts so as to give an honest and true performance of life, each time we work toward lifting the ban against our transcending and obliterating the gender role status quo by continually questioning and challenging standard conceptualization of gender roles, only then will we begin as individuals and as a society to experience what Truman experienced after he lifted himself from the manufactured dome of artifice: the warmth and brightness of a true sun, and the coolness and wetness of natural rain. Possibly, our society can then rid itself of at least some of the gun violence as well.

While most of the respondents claimed their "individuality," I perceived the opposite. They marched in virtual lock step in attacking me. It was as if they acted in unison like a school of Piranha fish going after an evening meal. After a short while, their names became virtually interchangeable from the words that followed.

Unfortunately, the vast majority of people who responded simply confirmed my initial posting regarding the patriarchal system on which our country persists by exemplifying the notion of the people who *want their guns simply because they want their guns*, without providing, for the most part, rational justifications. As I have indicated in past commentaries, they echoed one another about a supposed tyrannical government waiting to take away individual freedoms, and about invaders and "aliens" waiting to overrun their space, which only an arsenal of weapons could ever counter. And they asserted that I have the irrational fear of firearms, so-called *hoplophobia*.

My final comment on their website included the following:

> As you know, a very contentious debate is currently underway in our country regarding the role and future of firearms. Unless and until you develop substance over bluster, you will ultimately lose the debate since you don't know how to debate. Currently, you hold the balance of power in the public imagination, but this will be short lived if you don't revert from attack, threat, and dehumanization of your opponents to informed arguments. In the end, bullying never succeeds in getting bullies what they want.

References

AEI. (2016, July 11). 2016 Data Point: The gun control gender gap. Retrieved 9/14/2019, http://www.aei.org/multimedia/2016-data-point-the-gun-control-gender-gap/.

Casper, M. J. (2013, January 18). What we aren't talking about when we talk about gun control. *The Feminist Wire*. Retrieved 9/14/2019, https://thefeministwire.com/2013/01/what-we-arent-talking-about-when-we-talk-about-gun-control/.

Chemaly, S. (2016, October 5). Mass killings in the US: Masculinity, masculinity, masculinity, *Huffington Post*. Retrieved 9/14/2019, https://www.huffpost.com/entry/mass-killings-in-the-us-w_b_8234322.

Everytown. (2019, Auguest 27). Gunfire on school grounds in the United States. Retrieved 9/14/2019, https://everytownresearch.org/gunfire-in-school/#12594.

Flock, E. (2013, June 13). Gun owners still overwhelmingly white males. *U.S. News and World Report*. n.p.

Pew Research Center. (2017). Report: America's complex relationship with guns. 6/22/2017.

Pharr, S. (1997). *Homophobia: A weapon of sexism*. Berkeley, CA: Chardon Press.

Young, I. M. (2004). Five faces of oppression. In L. Heldke & O'Connor (Eds.), *Oppression, privilege, & resistance* (pp. 37–63). Boston, MA: McGraw Hill.

Chapter Twenty-Four

White Christian Male Privilege & Guns by the Numbers

A Pew Research Center (Parker et al., 2017) study found the highest rates of gun ownership in the United States are among Republican white Protestant Evangelical men. White men (48%) own a gun, compared to about a quarter of white women and nonwhite men (24% each) own guns, along with 16% of nonwhite women. In addition, people who live in rural areas own guns in higher proportions than residents of urban areas (46% and 19% respectively). Republicans and Republican-leaning independents are more than twice as probable to own firearms (44%) than are Democrats and people who lean Democratic (20%).

Across racial demographics, white people have the highest frequencies of gun ownership (36%), with blacks at 24%, and Laxinx at 15%. Approximately two-thirds of gun owners report they own more than one gun, with 29% boasting ownership or five or more guns.

Regarding religious affiliation, white Evangelical Protestants own guns at the highest levels (44%) of any religious group compared with U.S. residents overall (30%). They responded (44%) that they are satisfied with current gun laws, which is significantly above the total of 30% of the larger U.S. population. Only 32% of white Evangelical Protestants call for stricter gun control measure versus the majority (52%) of the larger U.S. voting populace.

Like the fundamental rights of life, liberty, and the pursuit of happiness, many individuals, Christian or not, believe they have a divinely given right to own as many firearms in all and any form they choose. For them, unrestricted access to guns equate to their freedom to life, liberty, and their pursuit of happiness. They believe in the notion of ruthless individualism while society be damned. It does not take a village to raise a child for them, but only a man and his wife alone independently.

Resistance to social change is and always has been their credo. We have witnessed the same as we moved from a largely agrarian society to industrial technologies, and then into the digital information age. Societies often do not transition smoothly in an environment free of conflict and backlash. They pervert the concept of "freedom" by linking it to the relatively unlimited access to firearms. If our nation does not impose common sense regulations on firearms ownership, life in the United States will become even more tenuous. And besides, where in the Christian testaments is it recorded that Jesus said: "Pack heavy and blow the SOBs away"?

But from where are Republican white Christian Evangelicals getting their advice since their testaments are contradictory at best. Christian pro-gun advocates often cite the Gospel of Luke, 22:36. "If you don't have a sword, sell your cloak and buy one," Jesus was said to have once told his disciples. While Christian gun control supporters quote Matthew 26:52, "Put your sword back in its place," Jesus said to him, "for all who draw the sword will die by the sword." And Matthew 5:39, "But I say to you, Do not resist the one who is evil. But if anyone slaps you on the right cheek, turn to him the other also."

It doesn't take a rocket scientist or Freudian psychologist to explain why Republicans, white men, and Christians represent the leading groups demographically in the rate of gun ownership and opposition to regulations on the firearms industry. (I would have stated that "It doesn't take a brain surgeon ... " but Ben Carson shot to bits that stereotype.)

Muslims, Jews, Sikhs, Hindus, and non-affiliates are being elected in greater numbers in local and state elections. Two high-profile Muslim women sit in the U.S. House of Representatives. And Republican white Christian men hold on even tighter to their guns. As women and people of color gain more social and economic power and fill the ranks of businesses in positions formally closed to them, Republican white Christian men hold on even tighter to their guns. As ethnic and racial demographics change to the point where trends indicate that white people will soon no longer constitute the numerical majority, Republican white Christian men – whether or not they define themselves as "white nationalists" or the like – hold on even tighter to their guns.

The days of wild West rugged individualism are over. Either we change our style of living to consider the common good, or else we will certainly and more quickly increase our chances of dying individually and as a nation. If you need to feel the pulsating heat of a throbbing weapon of war in your hands, join the military and serve your country, or go to a firing range where you can rent a riveting metal semen-shooting simulator to overcompensate for your penile insecurities.

If you wish to commune closer with your conception of the Divine, lay down your weapons, meditate, and begin truly to listen to the still and gentle voices well within yourself. If you need to better protect yourself and your loved ones, push for comprehensive firearms regulations and help to get these weapons of death off our streets, out of our schools and our homes.

The United States of America has no higher rates of mental illness than our peer nations, but no other comparable country suffers the casualties to guns as the United States. We must remember first and foremost that hate is not a mental illness. Additionally, it is shameful that our young people must undergo "active shooter" drills and carry bullet proof backpacks to school.

Our nation's soul has been polluted by the easy and increased availability of firearms as our environment has been polluted by the relatively cheap availability of fossil fuels. As a misbehaving and obstinate child who places themselves in harm's way by stepping too close to the edge of a high cliff or ventures so near a raging campfire that it singes their clothing but does not understand that it must move away, we as a society must place restrictions for the physical and emotional safety of our society.

The theory of a "Social Contract" developed as far back as ancient Greece. Though iterated, reiterated, and reformed by numerous philosophers and public figures, the foundations of this social contract stand on the premise that people live together in community with the agreement that establishes moral, ethical, and overarching political rules of behavior between individuals, groups, and their government in the formation of a civil society. A violation by any of the signatories – individuals, groups, governments – jeopardizes the very stability of that progress toward a fully civil society.

The ancient Greek philosopher, Aristotle, wrote his *Politics* (Greek: Πολιτικά, Politiká) whose title means literally "the things concerning the polis." A polis (plural: poleis) was the typical organization of a community in the ancient Greek world. "Politics" can be defined as the way people living in groups make decisions, and about coming to agreement so people can live together.

Politics rests on issues of power regarding having control over one's life and influencing others. People and groups holding power in influencing others must follow the axiom that bioethicists and healthcare workers follow: *Primum non nocere* ("First, do no harm").

Researchers have charted cultures as falling along a continuum with several variables, including Individualism versus Collectivism: the degree of support for and emphasis on individual goals versus common or collective goals. Most of these same researchers place the U.S. and many other Western nations on the "Individualism" side of the continuum

A Philosophy of Selfishness

"My philosophy, in essence, is the concept of man as a heroic being, with his own happiness as the moral purpose of his life, with productive achievement as his noblest activity, and reason as his only absolute."

Ayn Rand, Appendix to *Atlas Shrugged* (1957)

Ayn Rand has become the intellectual center for the economic/political/social philosophy of Libertarianism. She constructs a bifurcated world of one-dimensional characters in her novels. On one side, she presents the noble, rational, intelligent, creative, inventive, self-reliant heroes of industry, of music and the arts, of science, of commerce and banking who wage a noble battle for dignity, integrity, personal and economic freedom for the profits of their labors within an unregulated "free market" Capitalist system.

On the other side, she portrays the "looters" represented by the followers, the led, the irrational, the unintelligent, the misguided, the misinformed, the corrupt government bureaucrats who regulate and manipulate the economy to justify nationalizing the means of economic production, who confiscate personal property, who deliver welfare to the unentitled, the lazy, and who thereby destroy personal incentive and motivation resulting in dependency.

Welfare Ayn Rand terms "unearned rewards," while arguing for a system of laisse-faire Capitalism separating economics and state. In other words, Ayn Rand paints a world in which the evil and misguided takers wage war against the noble and moral makers. She bristled against some long-held notions of collectivism, of shared sacrifice and shared rewards. Rather, she argued that individuals are not and should not be their brothers and sisters keepers; that one must only do unto oneself; that one must walk only in one's own shoes and not attempt to know the other by metaphorically walking in their shoes; that personal happiness is paramount; the greatest good is for you rather than the greatest number of people. Ayn Rand's philosophical essence accords with the axiom, live and let live. She advocates for a "rational selfishness," and she titled one of her non-fiction books, *The Virtue of Selfishness* (1964).

"6 Pillars of Character"

The organization, Character Counts, enumerates its "6 Pillars of Character," as "core ethical values that transcend cultural, religious and socioeconomic differences." These Pillars are: Trustworthiness,

Respect, Responsibility, Fairness, Caring, and Citizenship. Breaking any of these essential pillars seriously jeopardizes the stability of the entire structure, whether that be the family, the group, the culture, the nation, or the world.

If anything brings down the United States, if this noble democratic experiment of government of the people, by the people, and for the people fails, it will not be through a foreign invasion. No! It will be the result of our neglecting any of the primary 6 pillars. It will be through the domestic virus of over-inflated self-interest rather than concern for community and the natural environment – an unbridled selfishness in the guise of "freedom" in the accumulation of more wealth and resources than any individual or family will ever need to sustain a high quality of life. It will be because too many individuals reject the notion that it truly takes a village to raise a child.

Reference

Parker, K., Horowitz, J. M., Igielnik, R., Oliphant, J. B., & Brown, A. (2017, June 22). *America's complex relationship with guns.* Washington, DC: Pew Research Center.
Rand, A. (1964). *The virtue of selfishness.* New York: New American Library.
Rand, A. (1957). *Atlas shrugged.* New York: Penguin Random House.

Chapter Twenty-Five

Violence, White Supremacy, & Video Games

White supremacist neo-Nazi bigots are engaging in online video "games" in which the aim is to murder Jews, LGBTQ people, and BIPOC people. The video assassins, attributed to "Wheel Maker Studios," are openly promoting from Christopher Cantwell and his far-right website. Cantwell is well-known as the so-called "Crying Nazi" (Marcin, 2017). Reporters recorded him weeping in jail to gain sympathy following his arrest as one of the organizers of the infamous "Unite The Right" rally in Charlottesville, Virginia August 11 – 12, 2017 where marchers carried Tiki Torches and changed Nazi slogans. A marcher killed a counter protested with his car. In the original video game, *Angry Goy*, according to the British newspaper, *The Jewish Chronicle*, the game's opening announcement reads: "There is only one solution … a Final Solution" (Palmer, 2018).

Angry Goy II states in stark terms:

> *Angry Goy II* is the season's hit game for White males who have had it with Jewish bullshit. Instead of taking out your frustrations on actual human beings, you can fight the mongrels and degenerates on your computer! Use guns, knives, pepper spray, and more! Lay waste to wave after wave of shit-dicks, shitskins, shitstains, and the kikes they serve.

Game players on one level infiltrate a gay nightclub called "LGBTQ+ Agenda HQ" and shoot naked gays. If that is not enough, another level of *Angry Goy II,* white supremacists shoot journalists inside their press offices at "Fake News Network."

To "Other" Is a Verb

When any society defines the "other" as less than human, as disposable, as dangerous, as predatory, that society invariably commits acts of violence and in some instances, genocidal extermination against those "others," and "to other" must be seen as a verb, as an action (Mackey, 1992).

- Jews othered as vermin, "race" polluters, super wealthy world dominating capitalists, and, paradoxically, radical communists,
- LGBTQ people othered as subhuman child molesters, sexual predators, vectors of infection,
- African heritage people othered as inherently subservient, intellectually inferior, lazy, sexually predatory, criminals,
- Latinx people othered as gang members, drug dealers, lazy, rapists, invaders,
- First Nations peoples othered as savages, thieves, murders, sexual predators,
- Asians othered as perennial foreigners, culturally dangerous, clannish,
- Muslims othered as terrorists, religious invaders, dominators,
- People with disabilities othered as frightening, defective, biological mistakes,

and the list continues given the times and the places.

The American Psychological Association has determined that violent video games present a risk factor for aggression. The APA Task Force on Violent Media (Calvert et al, 2017) reported that violent video games increased aggressive behaviors, thoughts, and emotions, and decreased overall empathy. No conclusive evidence was found, however, connecting these games with criminality.

Clubs, Pubs, & Bars

It is not random or coincidental that *Angry Goy II* centers its violence on an LGBTQ nightclub. As marginalized and often hunted people and having few other places to meet one another, clubs, pubs, and bars have been common meeting options.

Since the early to mid-19th century, a linear history of homosexuality, bisexuality, and gender non-conformity predominately in the West begins with the formation of a homosexual and gender non-conforming "identity" and a sense of community brought about by the growth of industrialization, competitive capitalism, and the rise of modern science, which provided people with more social and personal options outside the home (D'Emilio, 1983). It is only within the last 160 or so years that there has been an organized and sustained political effort to protect the rights of people with same-sex and more-than-one-sex attractions, and those who cross traditional constructions of gender identity and expression.

Even before the rise of industrialization, in England there developed the first documented fairly-organized network of men in the West gathering together for company and sexual encounters. From around 1700 – 1830, a series of houses or pubs, later called "Molly Houses," catering to the needs of these men were established throughout London. Some of the "Houses" consisted of private rooms in taverns, while others were in private homes. Many of these houses were raided by police, the men tried, and some were executed.

In the United States, homosexuality was illegal until 1962 when Illinois became the first state to decriminalize. In the 1930s, for example, laws banned homosexuals service in licensed bars in New York state. Penalties included revocation of the bar's license to operate. In Columbus, Ohio, for example, a law forbad anyone appearing in public "in a dress not belonging to his or her sex." It was not overturned until 1974. Some laws mandated the wearing of at least three articles of clothing traditionally considered "appropriate" to one's sex assigned at birth. In addition, the mere presence of homosexuals in a bar constituted a "disorder."

FBI Director, J. Edgar Hoover, warned in 1936:

The present apathy of the public toward perverts [homosexuals] generally regarded as 'harmless,' should be changed to one of suspicious scrutiny. The harmless pervert of today can be and often is the loathsome mutilator and murderer of tomorrow ... The ordinary offender [turned] into a dangerous, predatory animal, preying upon society because he has been taught he can get away with it (Hoover, in Anderson, 2017, p. 430).

Many believe that Hoover had a "relationship" with his longtime companion Clyde Tolson. Not until 2003 in *Lawrence v. Texas* did the Supreme Court strike down remaining laws against consensual adult same-sex sexuality.

Because LGBTQ people had few indoor options other than clubs to congregate, these spaces have been sites of harassment and violence.

- March 8, 1970: The Snake Pit Bar raid, New York City, an unlicensed bar with dancing and alcohol, a few blocks from the Stonewall Inn. Police took all patrons to a police station. One patron, Alfred Diego Vinales, a 23-years old Argentinian national with an expired visa threw himself from a window at the station to escape. He was impaled on the iron spiked fence below in five places on his body. Rescuers cut away the fence, and he was taken to hospital where he survived. The community organized a protest march around the raid.
- June 24, 1973: someone threw a Molotov Cocktail into The UpStairs Lounge in New Orleans, Louisiana killing 32 patrons.
- November 19, 1980: shots were fired outside the Ramrod club in New York City. No one was injured. The shooter yelled that gay men are agents of the Devil and were stalking him and "trying to steal my soul just by looking at me."
- February 21, 1997: a nail bomb exploded injuring 5 people at Other Side Lounge, a lesbian club in Atlanta, Georgia.
- April 30, 1999: a bomb went off at Admiral Duncan pub in London, England killing 2 and injuring another 81 people.
- September 22, 2000: a shooter opened fire at The Back Street Café in Roanoke, Virginia killing 1 person and wounding another 6.
- December 31, 2013: an arson fire on the gasoline-soaked carpeted stairway at Neighbours nightclub, Seattle, Washington. No injuries were reported.

- June 12, 2016: in the deadliest hate crime at an LGBTQ club, a shooter with a semiautomatic weapon and a handgun at Pulse in Orlando, Florida killed 49 and injured another 53 people who had been enjoying Latino night festivities.

What kind of country and what are the conditions that empower people to spray bullets into human bodies at Mother Emanuel AME Church, Tree of Life Synagogue, Pulse nightclub, and so many other places? What kind of a country and what conditions are conducive to empower people to produce and proudly promote video games like the *Angry Goy* series?

As the popular expression asserts that "Elections have consequences," and while the jury is still out, video games have consequences too.

References

Anderson, L. (2017). *Deviance: Social constructions and blurred boundaries*. Berkeley, CA: University of California Press.

Calvert, S. L., Appelbaum, L., Dodge, K. A., Graham, S., Nagayama Hall, G. C., Hamby, S., L. G., ..., Hedges, L. V. (2017, February-March). The American Psychological Association Task Force assessment of violent video games. Science in the service of public interest. *American Psychologist, 72*(2), 126–143

D'Emilio, J. (1983). *Sexual politics, sexual communities: The making of a homosexual minority in the United States 1940–1970*. Chicago, IL: The University of Chicago Press.

Mackey, N. (1992.) Other: From noun to verb. *Representations, 32*, pp. 51-70.

Marcin, T. (2017, August 31). Christopher Cantwell, the Charlottesville 'Crying Nazi,' wants your sympathy from jail. *Newsweek*, n.p.

Palmer, E. (2018, November 13). 'Angry Goy 2' Neo-Nazi video game lets users kill LGBT people and minorities to save Donald Trump. *Newsweek*, n.p.

Chapter Twenty-Six

Donald Trump as White Supremacist Radicalizer-In-Chief

Donald Trump depicted Latinx people in the language of disease, as infestation, as criminals, rapists, as ruthless drug gangs, as simultaneously lazy and as workers attempting to steal jobs from white people, and as breeders and invading hoards that if allowed to cross our boarders, will replace the white majority. Throughout U.S. history, rather than characterizing immigrants and refugees in humanitarian terms, many conservative and Christian white nationalists and nativists use narratives representing refugees as invaders, as barbarians at the gates who, if allowed to enter, will destroy the glorious civilization we have established among the "lesser" nations of the Earth.

The day Donald Trump descended the escalator in his tower of gold, with head raised forward like Benito Mussolini as if holding court at his press conference announcing his run for the presidency on June 16, 2015, he tossed down the bodies of Mexican people like red bloody Trump steaks as his initial steppingstones on his march to the White House. "[Mexico is] sending people that have lots of problems, and they are bringing those problems to us," he warned. "They are bringing drugs, and bringing crime, and they're rapists" (Schwartz, 2015).

Trump during his presidency subsequently placed the children of people attempting to gain refugee status into cages, he ordered a massive buildup of our military to "guard" the southern border from what Trump termed "invaders" from Central America, and he stated that he intended to eliminate the 14th Amendment's guarantee of citizenship status to children born in the U.S. when their parents were born elsewhere. The 2016 Republican Party Platform codified the language by defining the "other" as "illegal aliens," as if they were dangerous and deadly non-human raiders from deep space.

Trump was also a prominent and outspoken "birther." He consistently tried to define President Barack Obama as "other" by attempting to prevent our former President the right of self-definition – an apparent contradiction within a political party that emphasizes rugged individualism, freedom, and liberty.

Stereotypes & Scapegoats

A stereotype is an oversimplified, preconceived, and standardized conception, opinion, affective attitude, judgment, or image of a person or group held in common by members of other groups. Originally referring to the process of making type from a metal mold in printing, social stereotypes can be viewed as molds of regular and invariable patterns of evaluation of others.

Stereotyping can and often does result in singling out individuals and groups as targets of hostility and violence, even though they may have little or nothing to do with the offenses for which they stand accused. This is referred to as scapegoating. With scapegoating, people tend to view all members of another group as inferior and to assume that all members are alike in most respects. This attitude often leads to even further marginalization.

The origin of the scapegoat dates to the Book of Leviticus (16:20–22). On the Day of Atonement, the high priest selected a live goat by lot. He placed both hands on the goat's head and confessed over it the sins of the people. In this way, he symbolically transferred the sins of the people onto the animal, which was then cast out into the wilderness. This process thus purged the people, for a time, of their feelings of guilt, shame, and fear.

When stereotyping occurs, people tend to overlook all other characteristics of the group. Individuals sometime use stereotypes to justify the subjugation of members of that group. In this sense, stereotypes conform to the literal meaning of the word "prejudice," which is a pre-judgment, derived from the Latin *praejudicium*.

When demagogues play on people's fears and prejudices by invoking these images for their own political, social, and economic gains, in more instances than not, this results in loss of civil and human rights, harassment, violence, and at times, death of the "other." Throughout history, most dominant groups have depicted or represented minoritized groups in a variety of negative ways to maintain control or mastery. Dominant groups represent minoritized groups through myths and stereotypes in proverbs, social commentary, literature, jokes, epithets, pictorial depictions, and other hegemonic forms. Looking over this history, for example, we find many clear and stunning connections between historical representations of several minoritized groups, whom dominant groups construct as subhuman (lower "racial") life forms.

On the Jews

The German Nazis used similar language in its 1940 propaganda film *"Der Ewige Jude"* ("The Eternal Jew") representing Jews as plague-ridden hordes of rats. The Nazis accepted and advanced the "scientific" view that European-heritage Jews, in fact, all Jews of every so-called "race," constitute a separate and lower "race" as justification for extermination as if we were vermin. *The Eternal Jew* portrays Jews as spreading infection and degeneracy, which, if allowed to continue, would result in the eventual collapse of civilization and its institutions.

In this propaganda film, Jewish people were said to commit 47% of all robberies and to make up 98% of those involved in prostitution. "The Jews," according to the film's narrator, "are only one percent of the population" but they know how to "terrorize a great, tolerant nation" by controlling finance, the arts, education, and the media.

On one hand, Jews have been stereotyped as "super capitalists" whose inordinate wealth enables them to manipulate world banking systems and to control politicians and the media through well-financed lobbying campaigns. They are perceived as a "privileged class" highly educated and disproportionately represented in the "cultural elite." On the other hand, they are seen as radicals who are attempting to overthrow the capitalist system and the dominant culture. During the "McCarthy Era" at the height of the Cold War, for example, several U.S. Congressional leaders declared that Communists (associated in the public mind at the time with Jews) corrupted the minds of "good upstanding Americans" as well as the integrity of the governmental system, and, therefore, they must be purged from their positions.

During the Middle Ages, for example, Christians characterized Jews as having tails concealed beneath their garments and a peculiar smell. This led to reports that they were in the service of the Devil, actually that the Devil was their father. The "Judensau," an anti-Jewish motif that was used in medieval texts and even carved on several churches in Central Europe, depicted a Jew sexually entwined with a pig, sucking the sow's utter and eating and drinking its excrement.

Furthermore, a 13th-century law forwarded the idea that Jews were less than human by explicitly stating that Christians who had sex with Jews were the same as Christians who had sex with animals. The ravages of the Black Death throughout Europe, which wiped out an estimated one-fourth to one-half of the population in the 12th and 13th centuries were also blamed on Jews, who were accused of poisoning drinking wells.

Christians charged Jews with transmitting other diseases as well, most notably syphilis, which they referred to as "the Jewish disease" throughout Europe in the 19th century, even though the incidence of syphilis within the Jewish community had been no higher than in the larger population. Medical literature of the time alleged that syphilis was spread to newly circumcised Jewish infants through the practice of *metzitzah b'peh*, the sucking of the penis by the *mohel* (the ritual circumciser) to stop the bleeding. Fellatio thus became not only a marker of "perversion" but also a sign of the Jewish transmission of disease.

The Anti-Defamation League accused Donald Trump of "conjuring painful [antisemitic] stereotypes and baseless conspiracy theories" in his language and in his political ads. Jonathan Greenblatt, the organization's chief executive, wrote: "Whether intentional or not, the images and rhetoric in [Trump's] ad touch on subjects that anti-Semites have used for ages. This needs to stop" (Benen, 2016). In addition, the Anti-Defamation League found that in counties hosting a Trump rally in 2016 experienced a 226% increase in reported hate crimes.

Christian White Nationalism

On a more basic and personal level, the rhetoric of invasion taps into our psychological fears, or more accurately, terrors of infection: our country, our workplaces, and more basically, our private places in which "aliens" forcefully penetrate our bodies, into our orifices, and down to the smallest cellular level.

Modern day Christian white supremacists/neo-Nazis believe that only white Anglo-Saxon Protestant able-bodied heterosexuals have been granted a soul by God. Everyone else they refer to as "mud people," those without a soul and without meaning, value, or worth.

As hundreds of white nationalists lined the streets of Charlottesville, Virginia (August 11 - 12, 2017) to protest the removal of a statue of Confederate Gen. Robert E. Lee from downtown Lee park, some waved Confederate and Nazi flags, brandished shields, and marched with burning torches. They shouted racist, antisemitic, and homophobic slurs repeating "JEWS WILL NOT REPLACE US!" At one point, they loudly chanted in unison: "FUCK YOU FAGGOTS!"

What these white, mostly male, presumably heterosexual protesters have in common is a belief in a "white ethno-state" according to Southern Poverty Law Center Research analyst Keegan Hankes. He referred to the so-called "alt-right" or far-right movement as a "grab bag of right-wing ideologies."

"They believe that white people are being systematically replaced and that inheritance to their homeland is being taken away from them," Hankes told NBC News. "There's this belief that basically white people are being replaced faster than they can reproduce" (Compton, 2017).

While Hankes acknowledged that not all white nationalists are homophobic, he argued that the majority of right-wing extremists are "virulently anti-LGBT," and that they reveal an anxiety and obsession about white birth rates, which are just barely keeping pace with those of racialized minorities. Hankes asserted that many of these extremists may blame the birth rate disparity on the nationwide legalization of marriage for same-sex couples.

Politicians and most other residents of the United States alike, from every rung along the full political spectrum, generally agree on one issue: our immigration system is severely broken and needs fixing. Seemingly insurmountable gaps in political solutions to repair the system along with Congressional inaction to the point of blockage have brought the country to the point of crisis.

Though politicians and members of their constituencies argue immigration policy from seemingly infinite perspectives and sides, one point stands clear and definite: decisions as to who can enter this country and who can eventually gain citizenship status generally depend on issues of "race," for U.S. immigration systems reflect and serve as the country's official "racial" policies.

The murder of eleven Jewish congregants, and injury to 6 others, including 4 police officers at the Tree of Life Synagogue in Pittsburgh, and one woman at the Chabad Synagogue in Poway, California, in addition to a spike of 57% of reported antisemitic incidents in 2017 over just one year earlier, indicate that Jews and other marginalized groups remain at increased risk.

The murder of 19 primarily Latinx people and the wounding of dozens more at a shopping center in El Paso, Texas, the murder of 6 worshipers and wounding of 4 at a Sikh Temple in Oak Creek, Wisconsin, and the murder of 9 black congregants at Emanuel AME Church all attest to the rising tide of white nationalist terrorism in the United States. And, of course, we must include the deadly white nationalist terrorist insurrection on January 6, 2021 at the U.S. Capitol in Washington, D.C.

Donald Trump, this white supremacist terrorist Radicalizer-In-Chief, built his political career on stoking white grievance and nativist supremacy. As such, though he did not pull the triggers on the firearms of mass carnage, he is complicit in aiding and abetting these domestic terrorists. The Unite the Right rally, Charlottesville, Virginia brought together Christian white supremacists, members of the alt-right, neo-Confederates, neo-fascists, white nationalists, neo-Nazis, and far-right militias. They killed a counter-protester by plowing a car into the crowd.

"I think there is blame on both sides," said Trump about the rally. "You had a group on one side that was bad. You had a group on the other side that was also very violent. Nobody wants to say that. I'll say it right now." He criticized "alt-left" groups that he claimed were "very, very violent." He later stated that "There were very fine people on both sides." Donald Trump, through his actions and through the bullhorn of his rhetoric, moved the once right-wing political extremes front and center into the mainstream, and along the way, has empowered and enabled the hate and the haters to thrive.

Now a symbolic winter has come, the long night has come not only to Game of Thrones, but as it seems, to the United State. But a game it is not. Christian white nativists compete, react, slaughter for dominance. Prior wars are forgotten between these supremacists as they forge fresh alliances. They organize and search for power and treasure through divisions, never contemplating that sharing can supplant the ethic of divide and conquer, that peace can supersede war, that "power with" can surpass "power over." The White Walkers represent the collective unconscious, searching, tracking, coming for us. We can defeat them when we know ourselves, our pasts, our todays, when we imagine coming closer toward the conscious visionary thinkers we are and can still become.

No, this is no game at all. Rather it is a world's saga. We have come to a normalization of burying our dead as despots blare jingoist cries. We renounce our rights, our liberty for false promises of security. Authoritarians invent subversive invading nemeses to gain, maintain, and enhance their strangle hold, which threatens destruction from within the nation itself.

No, this is no game at all. It is, rather, a mirror, a cautionary tale, a glimpse into our tomorrows lest we alter, change, correct course, for we now stand at that existential cut-off point.

References

Anti-Defamation League. (2016). "H.E.A.T. map": Hate, extremism, antisemitism, terrorism report. New York.

Benen, S. (2016, November 7). Trump's closing argument faces allegations of anti-Semitism. *MSNBC*. Retrieved 9/14/2019, http://www.msnbc.com/rachel-maddow-show/trumps-closing-argument-faces-allegations-anti-semitism.

Compton, J. (2017, August 21). Why are so many white nationalists 'virulently anti-LGBT'? *NBC News*. Retrieved 9/14/2019, https://www.nbcnews.com/feature/nbc-out/why-are-so-many-white-nationalists-virulently-anti-lgbt-n794466.

Schwartz, I. (2015, June 16). Trump: Mexico not sending us their best; Criminals, drug dealers and rapists are crossing border. *Real Clear Politics*. Retrieved 9/14/2019, https://www.realclearpolitics.com/video/2015/06/16/trump_mexico_not_sending_us_their_best_criminals_drug_dealers_and_rapists_are_crossing_border.html.

Section Four

Activism

Chapter Twenty-Seven

Gays Against Guns & Pink Pistols

The United States ranks first among 178 countries in 2017 for the highest rate of firearms with 120.5 per 100 residents, the Falkland Islands coming in a distant second at 62.1, Yemen third at 52.8, and New Caledonia forth at 42.5 (Graduate Institute of International and Development Studies, 2017). Like individuals within most other social-demographically-constructed communities, LGBTQ people in the United States differ widely on issues of firearms along a continuum from imposing absolutely no restrictions on firearms ownership on one end, to fully repealing the Second Amendment on the other.

Two particular groups embody at least some of the diverse attitudes of individuals within our LGBTQ communities: "Gays against Guns" and "Pink Pistols." Toward one end of the debate, Gays against Guns' members and as a group are claiming: "Queer complacency is over." The group is calling for a multi-pronged approach to gun safety in order to "Thwart the life-threatening convergence of homophobia and flawed gun policy" (Rudin, 2019). Included among its goals: "to ban access to high-capacity magazine guns and assault weapons, create stricter background checks for gun owners, close the loophole that allows sales of weapons at gun shows without background checks, ban gun sales via the internet, and block people on the FBI watch-list from purchasing guns."

As other militant non-violent groups of the past, Gays against Guns conducts visible demonstrations to raise issues to the highest levels of public discourse like we did in the heydays of the Gay Liberation Front, Gay Activists Alliance, Women's Liberation, ACT UP, Queer Nation, and others. At the New York City Pride March on June 26, 2016 members shouted chants calling for firearms safety, as people then dropped to the ground in a "die in" to emphasize legislative inaction and silence.

Situated toward the other end of the firearms debate is Pink Pistols, a national group originally organizing in 2000, but whose membership has risen enormously since the Pulse nightclub shooting on June 12, 2016 killing 49 and wounding another 53. Like Gays against Guns, Pink Pistols understands the clear links between homophobia and violence against our community. However, unlike the other group, Pink Pistols' solution is not to increased gun regulations, but, rather, it advocates for increased gun ownership, including hand guns and pistols of any color, as well as high-velocity and high-magazine capacity rifles.

President of the Utah chapter of this LGBTQ pro-gun group, Matt Schlentz, was profiled in the *Salt Lake City Tribune* posing in front of his Rainbow Gadsen Flag (with the saying "Don't Tread on Me") and his AR-15, similar to the weapon used at Pulse, in his backyard in Salt Lake City. Minus the rainbow, the Gadsen Flag is the same one deployed to represent the right-wing political group, The Tea Party (Kane, 2016) and it was carried by some of the terrorist extremists at the Capitol insurrection on January 6, 2021.

Though upsetting enough as it stands, the article's title altered the empowering motto of Queer Nation from "We're Here, We're Queer, We're Fabulous, Get Used to It," to the perverted and corrupted paraphrase: "We're Here, We're Queer, And We're Packing Heat."

I stand fully on the side of Gays against Guns, which is attempting to reduce the number of weapons and the skyrocketing gun violence directed against LGBTQ and all individuals and communities. Though I understand the sentiment of taking up arms, I cannot support Pink Pistols' perspective. Unfortunately, rather than diligently working for common sense firearms safety measures, Pink Pistols colludes in the endless cycle of increasing firearms in this country. When one fights fire with fire, one gets higher and hotter flames, and we all get seriously burned.

This brings to mind the profound words of Audre Lorde (1984): "The master's tools will never dismantle the master's house." While Gays against Guns has picked up new and refreshed tools, Pink Pistols continues to employ the oppressors' tools crafted by the firearms industry and promoted and propagandized by the gun lobby and the National Rifle Association.

References

Graduate Institute of International and Development Studies. (2017). Small arms survey. Geneva, Switzerland.

Kane, R. (2016, July 4). LGBT community looks at self-defense. *The Salt Lake Tribune.* Retrieved 9/9/2019, https://archive.sltrib.com/article.php?id=4011110&itype=CMSID).

Lorde, A. (1984). *The master's tools will never dismantle the master's house. In Sister outsider: Essays and speeches.* Berkeley, CA: Crossing Press, pp. 110–114.

Rudin, J. (2019, August 7). Event Recap: When they take lives, we take the street. *Gays against Guns.* Retrieved 9/14/2019, https://www.gaysagainstguns.net/.

Chapter Twenty-Eight

Gays Against Guns Following Movement Traditions

Violence and the threat of violence comprise two of the many elements connecting the multiple forms of oppression. As marginalized people, we remain at risk of violence based solely on our social identities. Therefore, common sense firearms safety measures serve everyone, marginalized and dominant group members alike.

I felt enormous excitement and pride, but not particularly surprise, when watching on TV iconic civil rights leader, Representative John Lewis of Georgia, leading other courageous Democratic activists on June 22, 2016 by putting their bodies on the floor of the House to stand up for people of this country. These elected officials broke House rules to fix a broken legislative system controlled by corporate greed at the expense of real people's lives in failing to pass common sense gun safety measures that the vast majority of U.S. residents support.

Likewise, I experienced great excitement and pride, though again, not surprise, when learning of an action conducted by the newly launched LGBTQ gun control group, Gays Against Guns (GAG), at the 2016 New York City Pride March in which group members shouted chants calling for firearms safety, as people then dropped to the ground in a "die in" to emphasize legislative inaction and silence.

While members of our community voiced our concerns, proposed initiatives, worked with firearms safety organizations, wrote policy papers and editorials, and grieved each time we learned of another mass shooting and individual gun-related killings in inner cities, suburbs, and country sides, possibly the slaughter of innocents, primarily LGBTQ people of color at the Pulse nightclub in Orlando, were the bullets that finally broke the backing of the current legislative paralysis on gun safety measures. Maybe, just maybe, we have finally reached a critical mass in demanding that enough is enough!

GAG's reflexive (pun intended) decision to engage in non-violent direct action follows a tradition in the annals of queer political organizing. For example, LGBTQ people led in the fight to counter the rising AIDS pandemic in the 1980s and 1990s. Groups like the AIDS Coalition to Unleash Power (ACT UP) protested governmental, corporate, and larger societal inaction and literal silence.

By the time the impending HIV/AIDS epidemic hit, a grassroots network of LGBTQ social, political, and informational organizations had been put in place. Though liberation and civil rights organizing continued as before, the virus injected a new element into the political agenda. On a personal level, virtually everyone had been touched in some ways by the effects of the epidemic. A community-wide bereavement process began as the number of AIDS-related deaths increased.

Lesbians, gay males, bisexuals, transgender, and intersex people were on the forefront of a coordinated effort to provide care and support for people with HIV/AIDS. Existing gay and lesbian community centers expanded services, while establishing new centers dedicated to serving the needs of people with HIV/AIDS and their loved ones. We formulated safer sex guidelines to help slow transmission. Ironically, queers taught heterosexuals how to engage in sex more safely.

In March 1987, the direct-action group ACT UP formed in New York City largely by young activists. A network of local chapters quickly grew in over 120 cities throughout the world. Though independently developed and run, the network organized under the theme "Silence = Death" beneath an inverted pink triangle (turning upside down the insignia the Nazis forced men accused of homosexuality to wear in German concentration camps.) They reclaimed the pink triangle signifying the ultimate stigmata of oppression, and turning it into a symbol of empowerment, to lift people out of lethargy and denial and as a call to action to counter the crisis.

ACT UP groups, based on a philosophy of direct, grass-roots actions, conducted highly visible demonstrations, often involving acts of nonviolent civil disobedience in which participants on occasion placed themselves at risk for arrest and even injury. AIDS activists, which primarily included young people, not only challenged traditional ways that scientific knowledge was disseminated, but more importantly, questioned the very mechanisms by which scientific inquiry was conducted, and they even redefined the meanings of "science."

AIDS activists – including members of direct-action groups like ACT UP, AIDS educators, journalists and writers, people with AIDS, workers in AIDS service organizations and others – have won important victories on a number of fronts, including assisting people in become active participants in their own medical treatment, having greater input into drug trial designs, expanding access to drug trials, and expediting approval for certain drug therapies. In addition, Community Advisory Boards now hold pharmaceutical companies more accountable for the prices they charge.

Actually, all the major movements for progressive social change have many similarities and synergistic connections. Each has gained from the theorists, activists, and movement leaders who have preceded. The first wave of the Feminist movement in the 19th century of the Common Era gained its inspiration from the leadership and strategies of the Abolitionist movement. The workers and union movements built on the strengths of the Abolitionist and Feminist movements. The Civil Rights movements continued to build on those who went before. In fact, Dr. Martin Luther King, Jr. gained inspiration for his philosophy of non-violent resistance not only from his religious faith, but also from Mahatma Gandhi in South Africa and India, and Leo Tolstoy in Russia.

The second wave of the Feminist movement recharged from previous movements reflecting back to the first wave and also to the movements during the intervening years. The counter cultural youth movements,

the environmental justice movements, movements for peace, the lesbian, gay, bisexual, transgender, queer (LGBTQ) movements, the movement for intersex equality and rights, the disability rights movement,
the movement for medical and mental patients' rights, the movement
for youth liberation, indeed, the movements for all oppressed people
somehow connect and draw from one another.

Though the political and theocratic right accuses us of promoting
some sort of conspiratorial "gay agenda" on the people of our country, I have said not-so-ironically that whenever there are two LGBTQ
people in a room, there will be a least three different opinions. Even
the use of the term "queer" has been highly contested within LGBTQ
communities. Some lesbian and gay people don't consider bisexual and
pansexual people as part of their communities, while some LGB people
would rather trans people go away and form fully separate communities. Oy vey!

Just look at a few of the enormous array of groups and their "agendas": there are still gays for Trump, LGBTQ Marxists, Log Cabin
Republicans, there were LGBTQ people for Hillary, LGBTQ people for
Biden, Gays Against Guns (GAG) and Pink Pistols, LGBTQ members of
the National Rifle Association, LGBTQ anarchists, LGBTQ Catholics,
Sisters of Perpetual Indulgence, Ladies Against Women, Dykes on Bikes,
LGBTQ atheists, LGBTQ Muslims, lesbian daughters of Holocaust survivors, LGBTQ Bridge clubs, LGBTQ athletic clubs, Puerto Rican gay
men's organizations, black lesbians groups, groups for LGBTQ deaf
people and for LGBTQ elders, and yes, even LGBTQ members of racist
Christian white nationalist gangs.

So even though Identity Politics has served certain of our purposes
and has gained us selected victories, with the incredible diversity
within LGBTQ communities in terms of social identities and political
philosophies and outlooks, Identity Politics has shown its inherent lim-
itations. Therefore, its use can only take us to an incomplete point along
our multiple paths.

Though I continue to engage in Identity Politics occasionally on
particular issues, I have come to understand that sexual identities and
gender identities and expressions with the social oppressions that come
with these are simply not sufficient to connect a community, and by

extension, to fuel a movement for progressive social change. Therefore, my major focus and energy has been to join and connect with people of similar political *ideas* and *ideologies* that cut across individuals from disparate social identities in what some call "Idea Politics." My motto is: "I don't care who's in your bed. I care instead what's in your head!"

In this conceptualization of Idea Politics, people come together with others of like minds, political philosophies, and strategies for achieving their objectives. Though many differences inevitably remain, overall, we read from a similar if not from the same page.

Oppression operates like a wheel with many spokes in which each spoke represents one of the virtually endless systems of oppression. In a United States context, for example, individual spokes may represent oppression toward African Americans, recent African immigrants to this country, immigrants from Mexico and Central and South America, U.S.-born citizens whose parents immigrated from other nations, white women, trans women, gay men, Muslims, atheists, people along the autism spectrum, elders, youth, Spanish as first-language speakers, people outside the current socially-determined parameters of body size, and I could continue endlessly.

I have been joining with people who understand that if we work to dismantle only one or a few specific spokes, the wheel will continue spinning and trampling over people. We are working together toward dismantling all the many hideous spokes on the oppression wheel in our hopes of one day dismantling oppression in its totality.

So, if indeed it is true, as the old saying goes, that "the fish is the last to see or even feel the water because it is so pervasive," then from our vantage points at the margins or even outside the aquarium, queer people have a special opportunity – indeed, a responsibility – to serve as social commentators, as critics. Our experiences as outsiders give us the tools to expose and highlight the rigidity, the binary frames, of most social identity categories that flood and saturate our environment. We have the ability if we choose to use this to truly challenge the culture to move forever forward and to grow by looking beyond just ourselves.

Chapter Twenty-Nine

Youth Filling the Bucket to Tipping Point in Movement for Firearms Safety

> The people in the government who were voted into power are lying to us. And us kids seem to be the only ones who notice and our parents to call BS. Companies trying to make caricatures of the teenagers these days, saying that all we are self-involved and trend-obsessed and they hush us into submission when our message doesn't reach the ears of the nation, we are prepared to call BS. (Gonzalez in CNN, 2018)

Emma Gonzalez, a senior at Marjory Stoneman Douglas High School in Parkland, Florida excited the crowd at a gun control rally in Fort Lauderdale just four days after a gunman plowed down students and faculty with an AR-15 semi-automatic assault rifle killing 17 and injuring another 15 precious souls on February 14, 2018.

Through her voice, her passion, her outrage, and her deep commitment, Emma poured hot cleansing waters to the tipping point into a bucket representing a movement that has long been filling within our country to wash away the deeply entrenched stain of gun violence. It is a movement declaring that people are worth far more than corporate profits and political payoffs. It is a movement demanding that common sense measures be taken to finally begin to end the scourge that is gun violence in the United States of America. It is a movement proclaiming clearly and forcefully that condolences and prayers are simply not enough, and most importantly, that ENOUGH *IS* ENOUGH!

Emma continued:

> Politicians who sit in their gilded House and Senate seats funded by the NRA telling us nothing could have been done to prevent this, we call BS. They say tougher gun laws do not decrease gun violence. We call BS. They say a good guy with a gun stops a bad guy with a gun. We call BS. They say guns are just tools like knives and are as dangerous as cars. We call BS.

The United States stands at the cusp of great social change, led by strong and articulate young people who are cutting through the BS of longtime and largescale entrenchment holding in place a system catering to the rich and the well positioned. Black Lives Matter, and professional athletes sparked by the courageous actions of NFL star Colin Kaepernick are challenging institutional racism; women are pouring out into the streets and onto the ballots to break the log jam blocking their entry into the ranks of key policy makers; the Me Too and Time's Up Movements are standing up by demanding an end to sexual harassment and gender inequality.

Disability Rights activists are sitting in and acting up to ensure quality health care for all and the security of benefits for all who require them to maintain a high quality of life; LGBTQ people and their allies continue to push for full equality and the freedom to enter public facilities most closely aligning with people's gender identities; labor activists are demanding a realignment of the nation's economic priorities overwhelmingly and increasingly separating the haves from the rest of us.

And amidst it all, the youth, their radiant young faces catching the rays of the sun, marching side-by-side, hand-in-hand, their middle school, high school, and college groups, banners waving exaltedly in this storm of humanity, announcing their entry, their solidarity, their feisty outrage, and yes, their pride, chanting as if hit by an all-consuming revelation during these Trumpian and Post-Trumpian eras of retrenchment by shouting, "We're Not Going Back, We're NOT Going Back, WE'RE NOT GOING BACK!"

And indeed, they will not go back into those dank places of fear and denial that stifles the spirit and ruins so many lives. Oh, they will physically return to their schools and their homes. They will continue to study and play sports, to watch movies, listen to their iPods, text on their mobile phones, and write about their days on social media. Some will most likely continue to serve as community organizers, and some will go on to become parents, educators, and political leaders once their school days are behind.

The place they *will* go to, though, is nowhere that can be seen. It is a place of consciousness that teaches those who have entered that everyone is diminished when any one of us is demeaned; that gun violence as well as *all* the forms of oppression have no place in a just society.

From the adults in attendance at the Gun Control Rally in Fort Lauderdale beginning as a whisper and gaining to a mighty roar of support saying to the young people: "We are so glad you are here," came voices from the crowd. "We wish we could have stood up to the politicians, and gun lobbies and manufacturers when we were in school," cried others too numerous to count. "Thank you so much for your courage!"

Yes, it takes courage to speak out and counter the violence, the scapegoating, the fear of change, the ignorance, and yes, the hatred surrounding our lives. Fortunately, young people are developing positive identities at earlier ages than ever before. Activists of all ages are gaining selective electoral, legislative, and judicial victories.

Emma said: "They say no laws could have prevented the hundreds of senseless tragedies that have occurred. We call BS. That us kids don't know what we're talking about, that we're too young to understand how the government works. We call BS."

Young people have been integral in the development and success of social movements from the very beginning, and today, they are shaking up norms and traditions as have the young of the past. They are transforming and revolutionizing the society and its institutions by challenging overall power inequities, categorizations, and hierarchies, they are making links to the various forms of oppression, and they are forming coalitions with other marginalized groups.

Researcher Catherine Corrigall-Brown (2011), in her study of youth participation in social movements, found that activism is directly related with higher levels of self-esteem and self-efficacy, and also associated with verification and crystallization of identity development. Young people are dreaming their dreams, sharing their ideas and visions, and organizing to ensure a world free from all the deadly forms of oppression, and along their journey, they are inventing new ways of relating and being in the world. Their stories, experiences, and activism have great potential to bring us to a future where all people will live freely, unencumbered by constraining fears of being shot on their way to school, to work, or to the store.

We owe our gratitude to the young people throughout the decades who have taken the chisel to oppression and expanded the crack ever wider!

References

CNN. (2018, February 17). Florida student Emma Gonzalez to lawmakers and gun advocates: 'We call BS.' Retrieved 9/15/2019, https://www.cnn.com/2018/02/17/us/florida-student-emma-gonzalez-speech/index.html.

Corrigall-Brown, C. (2011). *Patterns of protest: Trajectories of participation in social movements.* Stanford, CA: Stanford University Press.

Chapter Thirty

Backlash Against Student Gun Safety Activists

Demanding "Never Again," "Enough Is Enough," and "March for Our Lives" to gun violence, and shouting "We Call BS" to the arguments against changing gun laws, a new generation of young people has been sparked into activism as a shooter's bullets cut down their peers and teachers at Marjorie Stoneman Douglas High School. Within a very short time, they have captured the imagination and admiration of those of us who have long hoped and fought for policy initiatives to bring an end to the senseless over-availability of firearms that kills tens-of-thousands of people annually in the U.S.

But as with all social movements for progressive social change, a strong and powerful opposition stands in the way. Member of the conservative political right, many who represent the interests of gun manufacturers and their lobbyists, have long engaged in and are continuing to wage war against gun safety advocates, even when, especially when, these advocates are young people.

During this Trumpian-inspired right-wing cultural moment within the context of declarations of "fake news," "conspiracy theories," "witch hunts," and verifiable distortions and lies in reaction to anything and everything reported that goes against their agendas and "values," the backlash to derail, by demeaning and impugning the integrity and motivation of these new youth advocates, was predictable in its speed and veracity. People in the extreme crevices of the political and theocratic right through many centrists accuse these young people of serving as pawns or coconspirators of the political left's anti-gun agenda, that they are mere puppets who have been coached what to say and how to say it.

On his radio show, Rush Limbaugh called out the student activists: "Everything they're doing is right out of the Democrat Party's various playbooks. It has the same enemies: the N.R.A. and guns" (Grynbaum, 2018).

Donald Trump Jr. took to Twitter to attack 17-year-old David Hogg, one of the student leaders from Marjorie Stoneman Douglas High School, for criticizing the Trump administration to protect his father, a former F.B.I agent. Trump Jr. referred to a YouTube video calling David Hogg an "Outspoken Trump-Hating School Shooting Survivor is Son of FBI Agent; MSM Helps Prop Up Incompetent Bureau" (Nashrulla & Smidt, 2018). Trump Jr. also admired a Tweet connected to an article by the far-right website, True Pundit, which referred to David Hogg as "the kid who has been running his mouth about how Donald Trump and the GOP are teaming to help murder high school kids by upholding the Second Amendment" (Nashrulla & Smidt, 2018).

The political right also refers to David and the other student gun safety activists as "crisis actors." During an interview with CNN's Anderson Cooper, Hogg responded to the charge: "I'm not a crisis actor. I'm someone who had to witness this and live through this, and I continue to be having to do that. I'm not acting on anybody's behalf" (Chavez, 2018).

With Douglas High School students observing from the balcony, Florida state legislators voted down, by a margin of nearly 2 to 1, a proposal to discuss the merits of banning AR-15 rifles in the state. And adding further insult to traumatic injury, Levi Patterson, the little league baseball team coach of 7- to 9-year-old 3rd graders in the town of Neosha, Missouri, has moved ahead in his planned raffle to fund his players despite growing criticism. The raffle winner will be awarded a new AR-15 rifle like the one used in the Florida tragedy (CBS News, 2018).

Backlash

In a General Electric TV commercial, "Ideas are Scary," a new-born and ultimately abandoned idea appears close to death in hospital. Somehow, though, it survives infancy into adolescence. As it ventures unwashed and homeless through the town searching for basic sustenance, it finds only harsh judgments, scorn, abuse, and rejection from people everywhere it goes. Then one day, by chance it stumbles upon the GE building, where people help it inside, support, and nurture it. Sometime thereafter, it walks out upon the bright stage of life where it has grown healthy and vibrant, with its beautiful multicolored plumage raised in brilliance and pride to a hearty and resounding ovation.

Yes, new ideas and the movements they spark have usually, at least initially, appeared messy and scary because they do, indeed, "threaten what is known," and because they truly "are the natural-born enemy to the way things are." In terms of ideas that challenge entrenched systems of power, oppression, and privilege, forces for the maintenance of the status quo often wage figurative and literal battles to exterminate counter ideas and actions to prevent and turn back any gains progressive movements have fought so tirelessly to advance.

We see history replete with intense and often violent backlash from many factions against movements working to end, for example, the dehumanizing and oppressive institution of slavery, apartheid in South Africa, human sex trafficking worldwide, and so-called "ethnic cleansing"; to advance women's suffrage and movements for women to control their bodies; to workers' rights; to the right to quality education and health care for all; to civil and human rights for people of color, for women, for LGBTQ people, for intersex people, for people with disabilities, for young people and elders, for people of all religions and for atheists and agnostics, for people of all ethnicities and national backgrounds, for equality of opportunity for people of all socioeconomic classes; and the instances continue endlessly.

Susan Faludi, in her now-classic exposé, *Backlash: The Undeclared War against American Women* (1991), details the intense resistance to feminist ideas and movements for gender equality. By shining a powerful illuminating spotlight on this backlash, Faludi reveals and debunks the myths and stereotypes perpetrated by social institutions, from business to the media, working to restrain women in all facets of their lives.

These young activists are quickly learning the lessons taught to anyone who risks taking a stand, especially when that stand challenges an entrenched and oppressive status quo. And through it all, these courageous committed young people are exhibiting poise, intelligence, and a righteous anger that will forever change them and our nation for the better.

Social Movements Theory

As defined by Killian, Smelser, and Turner (n.d.), a social movement is a loosely organized but sustained campaign in support of a social goal, typically either the implementation or the prevention of a change in society's structure or values. Although social movements differ in size, they are all essentially collective. That is, they result from the more or less spontaneous coming together of people whose relationships are not defined by rules and procedures but who merely share a common outlook on society.

Researchers have studied and charted the developmental cycles of social movements—how they arise, grow, and in some cases, recede. An early social movements scholar, Herbert Blumer (1969), charted four stages in social movements' lifecycles. His four stages were: Social Ferment, Popular Excitement, Formalization, and Institutionalization. More recently, researchers have furthered Blumer's work by distinguishing and renaming the stages as: Emergence, Coalescence, Bureaucratization, and Decline (Christiansen, 2009).

- **Stage 1: Emergence:** the initial stage of social movements in which there is very little or no organization, but, rather, widespread discontent or dissatisfaction on a single or several social issues or policies.

- **Stage 2: Coalescence:** stage two, also known as the "popular stage," is categorized with a higher degree of social discontent. Rex D. Hopper (1950) writes that at this stage "unrest is no longer covert, endemic, and esoteric; it becomes overt, epidemic, and exoteric. Discontent is no longer uncoordinated and individual; it tends to become focalized and collective….[and that] this is the stage when individuals participating in the mass behavior of the preceding stage become aware of each other (p. 273)." Leaders emerge and strategies for achieving their goals are discussed. This is the stage at which the Social Movement Organization (SMO) emerges. Strategies include mass rallies and inspirational speakers.
- **Stage 3: Bureaucratization:** In stage three, there are higher degrees of organization, leadership, and coordinated coalition-building strategies. Awareness has been raised and involvement has hit a point to the extent that trained staff with specialized knowledge must take on the daily functions of the organization to sustain it and not overwhelm the organizations' leadership and volunteers. At this stage, the SMO may have some degree of political power and the potential for social change (Macionis, 2001; Hopper, 1950).
- **Stage 4: Decline:** Social movements decline or recede for several reasons. Miller (1999) gives four reasons this can occur:
  - **Repression:** when authorities or their agents use repressive tactics such as violence to control or terminate a social movement.
  - **Cooptation:** when movement leaders relate or identify more with authorities or the movement's targets than with the social movement constituents.
  - **Success:** smaller social movements with clearly attainable goals (building a new community school, for example) most likely will decline after success has been achieved.
  - **Failure:** failure to attain its stated goals due to organizational and strategic weaknesses can result in the termination of social movement organizations. Miller (1999) give two primary reasons for such failure:

- **Factionalism:** when different factions or camps within vie for control and power
- **Encapsulation:** when internal conflicts deflect or implode the organization from the group's larger external goals
- **Possible Stage 5:** Macionis (2001) adds that social movements may also decline if as an organization, they become mainstream and part of the social establishment.

References

Blumer, H. (1969). Collective behavior. In Lee A.M., (Ed.), Principles of sociology (3rd Ed.). New York: Barnes and Noble Books.

CBS News. (2018, February 19). Youth baseball team to hold AR-15 raffle despite outcry. Retrieved 9/15/2019, https://www.cbsnews.com/news/neosho-missouri-youth-baseball-team-ar-15-raffle/.

Chavez, N. (2018, February 21). School shooting survivor knocks down 'crisis actor' claim. CNN. Retrieved 9/15/2019, https://www.cnn.com/2018/02/21/us/david-hogg-conspiracy-theories-response/index.html.

Christiansen, J. (2009). Four stages of social movements. EBSCO Publishing Inc. https://www.ebscohost.com/uploads/imported/thisTopic-dbTopic-1248.pdf

Faludi, S. (1991). *Backlash: The undeclared war against American women*. New York: Crown Publishing Group.

Grynbaum, M. M. (2018, February 20). Right-wing media uses Parkland shooting as conspiracy fodder. *New York Times*. Retrieved 9/15/2019, https://www.nytimes.com/2018/02/20/business/media/parkland-shooting-media-conspiracy.html.

Hopper, R. D. (1950). The revolutionary process: A frame of reference for the study of revolutionary movements. Social Forces 28 (3), 270-280. Retrieved May 12, 2008 from EBSCO Online Database SocINDEX http://search.ebscohost.com/login.aspx?direct=true&db=sih&AN=13582480&site=ehost-live.

Killian, L. M., Smelser, N. J., and Turner, R. H. Social movement, *Encyclopaedia Britannica*, at https://www.britannica.com/topic/social-movement, Accessed 5 July 2021.

Macionis, J. J. (2001) Sociology (8th ed). Upper Saddle River, New Jersey: Prentice Hall.

Miller, F. D. (1999). The end of SDS and the emergence of weatherman: Demise through success. In J. Freeman & V. Johnson, (Eds.), Waves of protest: Social movements since the Sixties (pp. 303-324). Lanham, Maryland: Rowman & Littlefield Publishers.

Nashrulla, T., & Smidt, R. (2018, February 20). Donald Trump Jr. liked tweets promoting a conspiracy theory about a Florida shooting survivor. *BuzzFeed*. Retrieved 9/15/2019, https://www.buzzfeednews.com/article/tasneemnashrulla/donald-trump-jr-conspiracy-theory-florida-shooting-survivor#.td3q4zEXZ.

Chapter Thirty-One

#MarchForOurLives & a New Generation of Truth Tellers

We can't solve problems by using the same kind of thinking we used when we created them.

Albert Einstein

While support and unqualified praise for the youthful leaders and participants of the March For Our Lives protest marches and rallies streamed in from virtually every continent on planet Earth, the naysayers perched from their alt-planet Hate and its satellite moons of Cynical, Irrational, and Assault attacking their efforts. As expected, the National Rifle Association mocked and demeaned March organizers and other survivors of gun violence. An NRA membership-drive video ran the caption:

Today's protests aren't spontaneous. Gun-hating billionaires and Hollywood elites are manipulating and exploiting children as part of their plan to DESTROY the Second Amendment and strip us of our right to defend ourselves and our loved ones (Griggs, 2018).

A video titled "A March For Their Lives" featured NRA TV host "Colion Noir" (a.k.a. Collins Iyare Idehen Jr.) who asserted: "From where I'm standing, it looks like a march to burn the Constitution and rewrite the parts that they don't like in crayon," referring to the youthful participants (NRA TV, 2018a).

In another NTA TV clip, Noir scolded the Parkland survivors, saying "no one would know your names" if someone with a gun had stopped the shooting at their school. "These kids ought to be marching against their own hypocritical belief structures," Noir continued. "The only reason we've ever heard of them is because the guns didn't come soon enough" (NRA TV, 2018b).

Representative Steve King (R-Iowa) shared a meme on Facebook attacking Douglas High School leader, Emma Gonzalez' Cuban heritage:

> This is how you look when you claim Cuban heritage yet don't speak Spanish and ignore the fact that your ancestors fled the island when the dictatorship turned Cuba into a prison camp, after removing all weapons from its citizens; hence their right to self defense (Hafner, 2018).

In fact, though, guns are not banned in Cuba. Fidel Castro headed an armed revolution against the government that involved citizens owning guns. Also, as my Jewish heritage does not depend on my knowing Hebrew, Cuban heritage does not depend on speaking Spanish.

Former Pennsylvania Senator, two-time presidential candidate, and CNN pundit Rick Santorum dismissed the demonstrations and their so-called "phony gun laws" from Hate's moon, Irrational, advising, instead, that if a violent shooter enters and injures people in the school, students should "do something about maybe taking CPR classes" (Watkins, 2018).

Santorum, who joined Donald Trump's Catholic Advisory Group to bring more Catholic voters to the campaign in front of the 2016 elections, opposed the leader of his Church's characterization of the recent worldwide calls for firearms safety in the United States. On the beginning of Holy Week leading to Easter, Pope Francis encouraged young people to keep speaking out and not allowing older generations to silence their voices or destroy their idealism. He said:

> There are many ways to silence young people and make them invisible. Many ways to anesthetize them, to make them keep quiet, ask nothing,

question nothing. There are many ways to sedate them, to keep them from getting involved, to make their dreams flat and dreary, petty and plaintive (Pullella, 2018).

And to his credit, Pope Francis touched on the importance of youth activism in bringing about social change, which has advanced societies throughout the ages.

Young people, with their idealism, honesty, and integrity still intact, those who are free from the constraints of traditions and entrenchments, of failed past solutions and dominant power structures, maintain the vision and abilities to think out of the proverbial box, to perceive different ways of thinking and being, of proposing and demanding in unity a new world of possibilities.

So, let the residents of planet Hate and its loons circulate around their own solar system. I choose to support and follow the courageous, passionate, and inspiring lead of this new generation of truth tellers who have exposed the full shining rays of the Sun.

References

Griggs, B. (2018, March 25). Here's what the NRA had to say today about the March for Our Lives. Retrieved 9/15/2019, https://www.cnn.com/2018/03/24/us/nra-march-response-trnd/index.html).

Hafner, J. (2018, March 26). Steve King campaign mocks the 'look' of Parkland survivor Emma Gonzalez in Facebook post. *USA Today*. Retrieved 9/15/2019, https://www.firstcoastnews.com/article/news/steve-king-campaign-mocks-the-look-of-parkland-survivor-emma-gonzalez-in-facebook-post/77-532320163.

NRA TV. (2018a, March 22). A march for their lives. Retrieved 9/15/2019, https://www.youtube.com/watch?v=3-6UuBk8HmU.

NRA TV. (2018b, March 22). Media Utterly Ignore Hero Who Stopped School Shooting. Retrieved 9/15/2019, https://www.youtube.com/watch?v=v-73kN20H4Q.

Pullella, P. (2018, March 25). Keep shouting, don't become anesthetized, pope tells young people. *Reuters*. Retrieved 9/15/2019, https://www.reuters.com/article/us-religion-easter-pope-palmsunday/keep-shouting-dont-become-anesthetized-pope-tells-young-people-idUSKBN1H10E3.

Watkins, E. (2018, March 26). Santorum: Instead of calling for gun laws, kids should take CPR classes. CNN. Retrieved 9/15/2019, https://www.cnn.com/2018/03/25/politics/rick-santorum-guns-cnntv/index.html.

Chapter Thirty-Two

Reflections of an AIDS Activist on Youth Gun Safety Movement

We're living through war, but where they're living it's peace time, and we're all in the same country.

This moving quote from Larry Kramer's play, *The Normal Heart* (1985) expressed how many of us felt throughout the early years of HIV/AIDS in the 1980s that amidst this crisis, officials and others in our country and throughout the world perpetuated a process of collective denial by refusing to acknowledge the mere existence of this war in their attempts to silence people with HIV and their allies.

Larry's quote came to mind recently as I watched the stirring voices of courageous young people taking to the podium shouting out impassioned words over loud speakers and bull horns, seeing young people falling to the pavement in front of the high black metal fences at the White House in symbolic death of a plague of gun violence prematurely killing so many, and hearing the cries and screams of parents and friends as they buried loved ones. I could not help but imagine so many, too many, parallels with the early years of the HIV/AIDS plague prematurely killing so many during the latter quarter of the 20th century.

Within each succeeding social movement throughout our history, individuals in consort with others chisel wide new openings by which people enter and become involved. Adherents to these movement pass through the entry points most consistent with their skills set, ideology, and comfort level. In both the movements to defeat HIV/AIDS and to reduce and eliminate gun violence, advocates have chiseled parallel entry points.

For example, in the fight for firearms safety, people are contacting legislators, writing letters and newspaper editorials, forming study groups, and are engaging in other creative ways to raise issues. Governmental and non-governmental organizations offer direct services including physicians, clinical trauma researchers and practitioners, and case workers. There are educators, fundraisers, funders, and sponsors of events, task forces and commissions investigating best practices.

In addition, several organizations promote education and engage in lobbying efforts such as The Giffords Law Center to Prevent Gun Violence, The Brady Center to Prevent Gun Violence, Moms Demand Action for Gun Sense in America, Everytown for Gun Safety, Gun Safety Alliance, Campaign to Keep Guns off Campus, and others. We see, as well, an increasing number of social media groups dedicated to raising awareness on gun safety. Selective politicians sponsor legislation, some of which have passed into laws in specific states.

Overarching themes of governmental and larger societal denial, deflection, inaction, recrimination, and distraction, coupled with a dereliction of duty falling in the zone of criminality from the power structure have made it a moral imperative as well as a survival strategy to organize for progressive and political social change.

In the social context surrounding both the AIDS and Gun Safety Movements, people in positions of power have rationalized their failures to take effective actions by framing gun violence as "mental health" issues, and AIDS as "lifestyle" issues of the deviant. Solutions have included "thoughts and prayers," arming more people with firearms, providing more mental health counselors, metal detectors, and with AIDS, changes in lifestyle, Christian conversion, tattoos on the buttocks of people with HIV, quarantine, *ad infinitum*.

When the power structure initially had its proverbial back against the wall and felt compelled to give something in an attempt to deflect and appease as minimally as possible, it offered, while possibly having no intention of carrying through, the scraps of "further investigating the problem," banning bump stocks, and extending background checks, and in the 1990s, allowing more people into clinical drug trials through "compassionate use" even though they may not have met the entrance criteria, funding free condoms, and permitting possibly one Person with AIDS (POA) on some policymaking committees.

The great abolitionist Frederick Douglass said in 1853, "If there is no struggle, there is no progress." The point he was making was that individuals, institutions, and societies virtually never relinquish even a bit of power without challenge and conflict. The mass murder by a fully-armed shooter at Marjory Stoneman Douglas High School in Parkland, Florida seemed to have provoked a tipping point ushering in the next development in a continuing movement to promote firearms safety in the United States: direct action led by a new generation of justifiably frightened and angry passionate young people, many of whom have grown up since and during the tragic murders of students at Columbine High School, Virginia Tech, and Sandy Hook Elementary School.

The parallels with organizing around HIV/AIDS could not be more striking. But first, as a caveat, HIV remains today a global problem as a global pandemic. As a social movement, though, it stands at a different place compared with the Gun Safety Movement. Throughout those early years of the plague, we had concrete and inspirational support from visionaries of times past and then present, marginalized people who worked throughout their lives to ensure a just and free society. These included German and British emancipation pioneers in the struggle for LGBTQ rights over a century before; leaders from the Women's Suffrage, Reproductive Freedoms, and Labor movements, and those who during past generations refused to accept the status quo – people challenging racial, ethnic, religious, and sexual inequalities; people standing up to protect the rights of women to control their bodies; people advocating for the health and working conditions of farmworkers, coal miners, seniors, people with disabilities, young people, and poor people; those fighting to halt the genocide of indigenous peoples, the

exploitation of workers in developing nations, the advancing encroachment of a nuclear winter, and the gradual and irreversible destruction
of our planet.

And why was the governmental response to HIV/AIDS so meager?
According to Randy Shilts in his book *And the Band Played On,*

> No one cared because it was homosexuals who were dying. Nobody came
> out and said it was all right for gays to drop dead; it was just that homosex-
> uals didn't seem to warrant the kind of urgent concern another set of vic-
> tims would engender .... Scientists didn't care because there was little glory,
> fame, and funding to be had in this field .... Nobody at the National Cancer
> Institute seemed to be in much of a hurry. The new syndrome clearly was a
> very low priority, even as it was becoming clear to more and more people that
> it threatened calamity (Shilts, 1987, p. 93).

In the face of this threat, we did not just sit back. We mobilized.
The women's health-care empowerment movement predates AIDS, as
recorded in the ground-breaking work, *Our Bodies, Ourselves* (Boson
Women's Health Book Collective, 1970). By the time the effects of HIV
were first felt, a grassroots network of medical, social, political, and
informational organizations had already been set in place. Some people, who under other circumstances would probably not have engaged
in political organizing, were spurred into activism by the crisis.

LGBTQ and heterosexual people were in the forefront of a coordinated effort to provide care and support for people with HIV/AIDS.
Existing LGBT community service centers expanded their services,
while new centers were established dedicated to serving the needs of
people HIV/AIDS: people of all races, socioeconomic classes, sexual
and gender identities, and their loved ones. These centers, sometimes
referred to as AIDS Service Organizations (ASOs), provided counseling, education, medical consultation and advocacy, legal and financial assistance, and guidance through the dizzying maze of local and
national agencies. Volunteer "buddies" assisted people with HIV/AIDS.
And trained volunteers staffed telephone hotlines to answer questions and refer people to local and national agencies, as they continue
doing today.

In addition, we must not overlook an irony. LGBTQ people developed safer sex strategies and educational campaigns and remain some of the leaders in prevention efforts. Just think about it: LGBTQ people teach heterosexual people how to decrease their risks of infection during sexual activity.

As important as all these initial organizing efforts were, some of us realized that we could advance only so far given the enormous backlash, and that we must do so much more to directly confront the crisis. We charged the government with being unconcerned with the epidemic because the majority of HIV-related cases existed in what we called "The 4-H Club": Homosexuals, Haitians, Heroin users, and people with Hemophilia – 3 of 4 groups that our society considered disposable. We also faulted the very system on which U.S. medicine was based, and we declared that clinical drug trials and drug distribution procedures as then constructed were inhumane.

Subsequently, by 1987, militant groups known as ACT UP (AIDS Coalition to Unleash Power) organized under the banner "Silence = Death." "We are a nonpartisan group of diverse individuals united in anger and committed to direct action to end the AIDS crisis," and so began another meeting of ACT UP chapters throughout the U.S., Canada, Europe, and Australia. Updating 1960s-style movement strategies, ACT UP groups challenged what we regarded as an intransigent government, arrogant medical establishment, greedy pharmaceutical and insurance industries, and a frightened and apathetic populous. We also fought against the internalized oppression within our own communities.

A new era dawned March 24, 1987 when a handful of furious and committed AIDS activists staged a sit-in at rush hour on Wall Street in protest of what they saw as foot-dragging by the U.S. Food and Drug Administration in withholding approval of promising HIV drugs, and price gauging by pharmaceutical companies: in particular Burroughs-Wellcome, which charged up to $13,000 per year for its antiviral, AZT: a drug, by the way, developed at public expense, and the Illinois-based Lyphomed Corporation for its pricing of pentamidine, a prophylaxis for pneumocystis carinii pneumonia.

The following October, over half a million people descended on Washington, DC as part of the National March for Lesbian and Gay Rights. Out of the March grew a unique coalition concerned with several progressive issues, though focused on AIDS. A new umbrella organization called ACT NOW (AIDS Coalition To Network, Organize, and Win) oversaw communications and planed actions on a national scale.

Based on a philosophy of direct, non-violent action, ACT UP members conducted highly visible demonstrations often involving acts of civil disobedience in which participants often placed themselves at risk for arrest. Dramatic and creative visuals were often used to garner media and public attention. ACT UP's agenda included pushing for greater access to experimental drugs and a streamlining of the drug trials process; decentralized drug trial processes in which subjects and their physicians determine cooperatively the most appropriate trial drug treatment; ensuring that third-party payers cover the costs of drugs once medical consensus has been reached rather than waiting for the FDA to conclude its paper chase; an end to inhumane placebo trials; expanded informed consent to guarantee all drug trial subjects the right to results, even preliminary, from trials in which their participation has made possible.

We also argued that People with AIDS must be represented on the Institutional Review Boards of every HIV/AIDS drug trial; allowing concurrent prophylactic treatment to anyone participating in drug trials; fair pricing of drugs by the pharmaceutical companies, and access to their books to justify the prices they charge; clean needle exchange programs; treatment for drug addiction on demand; and of enormous concern, universal access to health care.

In addition, we pushed for national anti-discrimination laws in terms of HIV status and sexual identity; protecting against mandatory HIV testing and quarantining; insurance and social security benefit protections; job and housing protections; freedom of immigration; and treatment for all incarcerated persons. This agenda was controversial and, indeed, ACT UP and its tactics were often criticized, even from within the ranks of the larger LGBTQ community. ACT UP, however, lists several victories to its credit, though history will have to be the final judge of its ultimate effectiveness.

When looking back over the history of HIV, one thing seems certain. LGBTQ people have been in the forefront of organizing since physicians first recognized the syndrome. We are there now working on the frontlines and we will continue to be there giving our knowledge, our compassion, our funds, and our energy until HIV no longer poses a significant threat to the health of *anyone* on this planet. Also, in areas of health outside HIV, our leadership, creativity, and commitment has helped people in so many ways.

I am reminded of the poignant words of Harry Hay, one of the founders of the Mattachine Society – a gay organization established first in Los Angeles during the 1950s – and the Radical Faeries – a queer spiritual movement. Hay believed that those of us in the LGBTQ community possess a special "gay sensibility" giving us a unique vision, a creative spirit that, if allowed to thrive unimpeded, can bestow remarkable benefits on society. Unfortunately, because of the oppressive environment in which most of us are forced to live, he concluded,

> We pulled the ugly green frog skin of heterosexual conformity over us, and that's how we got through high school with a full set of teeth. We know how to live through their eyes. We can always play their games, but are we denying ourselves by doing this? If you're going to carry the skin of conformity over you, you are going to suppress the beautiful prince or princess within you (Timmons, 1990, p. 265).

I would go further than Harry, though, by asserting that each of us, from all backgrounds and identities, have within us a unique vision and creative spirit. So, in these challenging times, whether around issues of gun violence, or elsewhere, if you find yourself beginning to pull that ugly green frog skin of conformity and apathy over your head, look in the mirror and scrub it away. By so doing, you will be pushing the boundaries ever further from the center. Your vision can create a new tomorrow, a safer and more just tomorrow, a tomorrow where we will see the end to the list of names on the AIDS Memorial Quilt, and where we will cease inscribing names on the directory of people cut down by violence in all its forms, in a tomorrow that is truly better and more equitable than today.

References

Boston Women's Health Book Collective. (1970). *Our bodies, ourselves*. New York: Touchstone Books.

Douglass, F. (1853). If there is no struggle, there is no progress. Black Past (2007, January 25). Retrieved 9/15/2019, https://www.blackpast.org/african-american-history/1857-frederick-douglass-if-there-no-struggle-there-no-progress/.

Kramer, L. (1985). *The normal heart*. New York: Samuel French, Inc.

Shilts, R. (1987). *And the bank played on: Politics, people, and the AIDS epidemic*. New York: St. Martin's Press.

Timmons, S. (1990). *The trouble with Harry Hay: Founder of the modern gay movement*. Boston, MA: Alyson Publications.

Chapter Thirty-Three

Young Gun Safety Advocates Walking Out & Changin' the Times

A new generation of young social and political activists poured out of their schools around the country on Wednesday, March 14, 2018, to mourn and to protest the senseless loss of 17 innocent beautiful souls cut down by a shooter exactly one month earlier at Marjory Stoneham Douglas High School.

Like those of us chronicled by then 23-year-old poet laureate Bob Dylan of an earlier generation during another defining historical moment, these new social warriors too gathered around people to give testimony on the tragedy of firearms violence by demanding that legislators and others in positions of power "start swimmin' or they'll sink like a stone."

At 10:00 in the morning, the call was given for 17-minutes of silent meditation in remembrance of the 17 murdered comrades. Speakers then contributed their voices in demanding the right to safe schools and safe streets free from the plague of violence long overtaking our nation. Following some rallies, students and their supporters marched to local parks to join with community members, or to government houses to meet with legislators. Demonstrators in Washington, DC sat with turned backs on the White House in silence, before marching in solidarity to the U.S. Capitol to lobby lawmakers.

Many school administrators viewed these rallies as learning opportunities for students actively to engage in the civil project of our democracy by adding their voices and their talents for constructive social change. Others, however, did not heed the call by figuratively standing in the doorway and blocking the hall.

Administrators at Saint Pius X Catholic High School in Atlanta, Georgia, for example, launched email messages and warned students over the intercom system that any student who engaged in the walk-out faced severe disciplinary action, including school suspension as ordered by the Catholic Arch Diocese.

Three female students from Saint Pius X High School spoke on camera with a reporter from MSNBC during the rally at a local Atlanta public school giving reasons why they defied their administrators and placed themselves at risk to add their voices of support in demanding their rights to safe schools. The young women had attempted to organize a similar rally at their Catholic school. When administrators rejected their request, they all agreed that they had to stand up and speak out with their voices and their bodies. Stated one: "This is a day I will remember for the rest of my life." All three acknowledged that they were taking risks by showing up, but they were certainly willing to take these risks.

As an undergraduate student, I attended San José State University from 1966 to 1969, and 1970 as a graduate student. San José State at that time had a relatively progressive administration. We had freedom of political speech, we organized and staffed informational tables throughout the campus, we had access to university facilities to hold our meetings and rallies. In fact, I was a chief organizer of a rally in support of our university president against criticism coming from some of the more conservative members of the state university board who considered our president too "tolerant" of campus anti-war and anti-racism protests and protesters.

Nonetheless, during the fall of 1967 and then again in 1968, we called for a student strike of classes. The purpose of the boycott was not to demonstrate against or criticize our professors, or even our university.

It was, rather, to send a message to our leaders in government – state and national – that the war we were waging in Vietnam was wrong, that it was misguided, that it was illegal according to international law.

I will never forget sitting in Botany class the week prior to the first planned strike, when Professor Thaw forthrightly threatened to give an in-class quiz on the day of the strike, and anyone absent that day would receive an automatic "F" on the quiz with no possibility of a make-up. To this day, I do not know where my courage came from as I raised my hand and stated that "This is one 'F' I would be proud to earn." To my utter amazement, other students cheered, and eventually Professor Thaw rescinded his threat.

By boycotting classes, students take a risk – however small at the time – but a risk nonetheless. And this is one of the, if not *the*, major points in the philosophy of civil disobedience. For it to be truly meaningful, for it to be a truly beneficial, life changing experience for the individual, there must be some aspect of risk and sacrifice; one must give something, pay something, in order to keep and to strengthen one's principles and one's sense of personal integrity.

My questions are thus: Will a person gain more, learn more, commit more to an idea or a cause if it is given to them freely or, rather, if they must risk something for it? Will the experience be more meaningful if one attends a rally between classes or if one puts one's principles on the line – and be willing to accept the consequences – to walk out or strike classes?

Schools are microcosms of the larger society. By students saying that "we will collectively take a stand," they are, a least symbolically, lodging their vote against what they believe to be an unjustifiable stand on the part of their government or by other leaders. They are declaring their opposition to politics and policies as usual. Let us remember that three young people helped to set the stage for the relative political freedoms youth enjoy today.

The Supreme Court of the United States handed down a landmark freedom of speech case for students on February 24, 1969. It involved two Des Moines, Iowa high school students, John Tinker, 15, and Christopher Eckhardt, 16, and John's 13-year-old sister, Mary Beth Tinker, a Des Moines junior high school student.

In December 1965, John, Christopher, and Mary Beth attended a meeting with a group of adults and other students in Des Moines at the Eckhardt's home. The purpose of the meeting was to come up with strategies whereby they could publicize their objections to the hostilities in Vietnam. They came up with an idea to express their support for a truce between the warring parties by wearing black armbands during the holiday season and by fasting on December 16 and New Year's Eve.

Meeting participants had previously engaged in non-violent activities to work toward ending the war, and they decided to join the program. When Des Moines school district officials learned of the proposed activity, on December 14 they adopted and distributed a policy stating that any student found wearing a black armband, and failing to remove it on request, would be suspended from school and allowed to return only without the armband. John, Christopher, and Mary Beth wore black armbands to school in violation of the stated policy, and school officials sent them home. Parents of the students petitioned the United States District Court to issue an injunction to school officials from disciplining the students, though the court dismissed the complaint on grounds that the school district had the right to take its actions to prevent breaches of school discipline.

On appeal to the United States Supreme Court, the justices ruled in favor of the students and against the school district in that the wearing of armbands for the purpose of expressing views is considered as a symbolic action, according to the court, "closely akin to 'pure speech'," and well within the Free Speech clause of the First Amendment and the Due Process Clause of the 14th Amendment. In addition, the Court found that school officials failed to prove that the wearing of the armbands would substantially disrupt school discipline. Speaking for the 7 to 2 majority in the case, Justice Abe Fortas wrote: "...In the absence of a specific showing of constitutionally valid reasons to regulate their speech, students are entitled to freedom of expression of their views." This case would have implications for numerous cases that followed.

Our society is constructed in such a way as to deny voice to young people in the decision-making process in the affairs of state. Young people do not hold powerful positions in the executive suites in business and industry, in media outlets, in the halls of Congress. Their strength, however, exists when they take collective action. Government leaders then begin to listen. In their collective strength, they can and have changed the world for the betterment of all.

Chapter Thirty-Four

Proposals for Reducing Gun Violence

Sports fans who have ever attended a live home game know of and most likely own a humongous foam hand glove with one finger raised high as they chant in unison that "We're Number One," "We're Number One," whether this is actually true. Well, fans of firearms in the United States of large military-style simi-automatic rifles to small pistols have taken aim on and have long held the number one ranking in the world in carrying the most civilian-owned firearms per capita of any other nation with 120.5 per 100 people (Small Arms Survey 2017). Collectively as a nation, we are number one in accumulating the most firearms of any place on Earth. With only an estimated 4.43% of the world's population, a United Nations study (2018) showed that ownership in the U.S. equals approximately 40% of the world's civilian-owned firearms population. Of an estimated total of 857 million guns owned by civilians in the world, residents of the United States own 393 million (AFP 2018).

Yes, indeed, we are number one! But this is not a record we should cheer. No trophies must be given in this home game that for so very often results in death, sudden or not. The United States far exceeds all of our peer nations in the highest rate of homicides per year with 29.7 per million residents (Zarracina 2015).

During the Covid lockdown in 2020, one could reasonably assume that gun-related deaths might have declined. This assumption, however, is wrong. Gun violence took the lives of approximately 20,000 U.S.-Americans, which surpassed any other year in the past two decades (Gun Violence Archive). An additional 24,000 people terminated their lives in gun-related suicides (Thebault & Rindler 2021).

While campaigning and after taking office, Joe Biden and Kamala Harris committed to pass gun safety reforms like, for example, universal background checks for all firearms sales public and private and the banning of assault-style weapons. Though polling results show that background checks are nearly universally supported – 97% including 97% of gun owners -- and 67% of those polled support a ban on the sale of assault rifles (Quinnipiac 2018), with the continuing and entrenched resistance within the Republican Party, the chances for common sense gun safety regulations remains slim.

Following the deadly insurrection on the U.S. Capitol on January 6, 2021, all Senators and House Representatives and their staffs should truly understand on the intellectual and emotional levels what their constituents experience daily across this nation. Republicans, though, spew the constant claims of the gun lobbyists and most ardently obsessed firearms fans that the parameters of the Second Amendment are vast, and that Congress must not place any limits on their purported God-given rights and freedoms to carry. But what about the people's rights to go to school, to work, to shop, to see a movie or live theater, to attend an open-air concert, and to take a walk without fearing they will be killed by someone with a gun? What about our rights to life, liberty, and the pursuit of our happiness?

June has been designated "Gun Violence Awareness Month," with June 1st as "Gun Violence Awareness Day." The first day and throughout the month are intended to raise awareness of the estimated 96+ people killed every day and the many more injured across the United States. We wear orange to symbolize the epidemic of gun violence ravaging the country. Throughout the month, organizations plan educational efforts, voter registration drives, and mobilization activities.

We currently live within a neo-liberal political climate in which national, state, and local governments are increasingly dismantling regulations for the benefit of the corporate sector's bottom line rather than to better ensure the safety and health of the people. While no single or a combination of measures will eliminate firearms deaths and injuries, several policy proposals that challenge the deregulatory trend can substantially diminish the plague of violence:

- Ban and criminalize the sale and possession of semi-automatic and so-called "assault" weapons!
- Pass universal background checks to close loopholes in the current system!
- Ban the purchase of firearms from those on the federal "no-fly" list, anyone convicted of domestic violence, and anyone who has a restraining order against them!
- Fully repeal the Dickey Amendment passed by Congress in 1996 mandating that "none of the funds made available for injury prevention and control at the Centers for Disease Control and Prevention may be used to advocate or promote gun control"!
- Increase funding for research investigating the causes and solutions of firearms violence!
- Strengthen the ban on the purchase of firearms and ammunition on the internet!
- Permanently ban so-called "Bump Stocks" and other technologies that increase the speed or force of semi-automatic weapons!
- Initiate background checks each time an individual purchases ammunition!
- Limit the number of firearms any individual can own!
- Limit the number of bullets any firearm magazine can hold!
- Limit the purchase of any firearm to the age of 21 (preferably 25) and above!
- Ban and criminalize the purchase and possession of "armor piercing" bullets, and hollow-tip bullets!
- Ban so-called "ghost guns," which are kits that include gun parts the owner assembles into a completed firearm!
- Initiate an anonymous reporting system for persons wanting to report suspicious behaviors of those who possess firearms!
- Investigate and initiate effective anti-bullying policies in schools and workplaces!

- Assess all incidents and continually update training procedures of law enforcement agencies on the national and local levels to better ensure equitable and bias-free policing in the community in which they are meant to serve!
- Substantially increase federal and local funding of mental health services and drug treatment!
- Require all firearms owners to take and pass a course in the proper use, safety, and storage of their weapons!
- Require firearms to contain a safety device designed to prevent the discharge of the weapon by accident or by unauthorized users!
- Rethink the "logic" of permitting concealed weapons, especially in places like houses of worship, colleges, bars, restaurants, and political rallies!
- Interface all data bases monitoring firearms ownership to assess and monitor the firearm-owning population more accurately and effectively!
- Institute ongoing gun buyback programs in towns and cities across the country!
- Pass "Red Flag Laws" allowing judges to issue an extreme risk protection order, which temporarily bans a person from owning a firearm if family or others near to the person can show they are a danger to themselves or others!
- Institute implicit bias trainings in schools, workplaces, and to reduce the incidents of the disproportionate violence toward people of color!
- Provide free or affordable anger management trainings for people who need these programs!
- Run for office and vote for candidates committed to passing gun safety regulations!
- Support measure to reduce the rates of poverty and hunger, and reform the tax system eliminating loopholes for the rich to avoid paying their fair share!
- Hold gun shop owners liable when selling firearms and ammunition to anyone who is not legally eligible to own, such as minors, felons, or people with a history of serious mental illness!

And I pose a critical question: Should gun manufacturers remain exempt from liability? In 2005, the U.S. Congress passed the Protection of Lawful Commerce in Arms Act shielding manufacturers and sellers from claims in civil courts brought by victims of gun violence.

As we all know, though, the chances for comprehensive common-sense gun reform in the United States is only a pipe dream as long as the gun lobby remains strong, even with the downturn of fortunes of the once might National Rifle Association. Nevertheless, this utter stupidity in our system of firearms laws must end. Enough is enough is enough is enough already! Actually, it is far past that time!

References

AFP (June 18, 2018). Americans own 40 percent of world's firearms: study. Retrieved March 25, 2021: https://news.yahoo.com/americans-own-40-percent-worlds-firearms-study-173747656.html

Gun Violence Archive. (March 15, 2021). Gun Violence Report Statistics for 2020. Retrieved March 25, 2021: https://www.gunviolencearchive.org/past-tolls.

Quinnipiac University Poll (2018). U.S. support for gun control tops 2 – 1: Highest ever. Retrieved March 25, 2021: https://poll.qu.edu/national/release-detail?ReleaseID=2521

Small Arms Survey (2017). Ranking by country for civilian-held firearms in per 100 population. Retrieved March 25, 2021: https://en.wikipedia.org/wiki/Estimated_number_of_civilian_guns_per_capita_by_country

Thebault, R. & Rindler, D. (March 23, 2021). Shooting never stopped during the pandemic: 2020 was the deadliest gun violence year in decades. *Washington Post.*

Zarracina, J. (June 20, 2015). These graphics show just how much of an insane outlier is on guns. Vox. Retrieved: March 25, 2021: https://www.vox.com/2015/6/20/8544507/gun-murders-ownership-charts

Chapter Thirty-Five

On Gun Violence: Uttering the Unutterable

I love life, and I love the people of my country far far far more than I value the "freedom" to bear arms. I don't know if any "reforms" will really solve the problems of gun violence in the United States. In all actuality, I believe we *must* repeal the Second Amendment now!

There! I uttered the unutterable, the ultimate taboo in U.S. political discourse.

As the horse once served as a primary means of transportation in earlier times, it now grazes and prances peacefully on rich pastures. Possibly during former moments in our history, we may have had reason to enact and enforce the Second Amendment of our great Constitution, but those bygone days have long since passed. Now we must put the Second Amendment out to pasture.

I believe that even our brilliant and well-meaning, but flawed founders did not want unlimited and unrestricted rights of firearm ownership. They could never have imagined the enormous leaps and heights to which the Second Amendment now menaces not only the very lives of our people, but more poignantly, how it imposes an existential threat to our nation.

Even if our early leaders had advocated for unrestricted gun ownership, these are the same men who owned and marketed enslaved Africans, committed genocide against and expelled native peoples, withheld enfranchisement from women, engaged in and killed one another in duels, and so on. Since those early times, legislation, judicial actions, and constitutional amendments have at least attempted to redress those past tragedies. Though we can never bring back the estimated 30,000 victims of gun violence each year, by gutting the Second Amendment we can give our residents a greater chance at life.

I often travel abroad visiting cites and people around the world. Increasingly during my journeys, people express to me that they admire the remarkable achievements and wonders of the United States, but because of the perennial gun violence, they vow not to step foot on this land. These same people believe they have more freedoms in their countries with severe firearms restrictions than we could ever have under our Second Amendment. And because of their well-founded hesitations to visit our country, they will never experience our gleaming cities, our fertile plains, our lush grasslands, our majestic mountains and national parks, and yes, our seemingly endless supply of shops. In the end, the realities of gun violence in the U.S. hurts everyone everywhere, with the possible exception of our enemies who desire to witness us defeated from within.

Rather than working to reduce the supply of firearms on our streets and in our homes, gun sales and ownership steadily increases. The United States ranks number 1 of 178 countries highest rate of firearms (Graduate Institute of International and Development Studies, 2017).

What will it take for us to cease fighting stupidity with stupidity? How many more of our precious people of all ages will have their lives cut short under the banner of "freedom to bear arms"? What will it take for us to reverse the unholy alliance between corporate America and powerful pressure groups controlling politicians in the service of firearms manufacturers? When is enough, enough?!

Reference

Graduate Institute of International and Development Studies. (2017). Small arms survey. Geneva, Switzerland.

Chapter Thirty-Six

Sing Along: "Let's Go Buy a Gun"

Lyrics by Dr. Warren J. Blumenfeld

Sung to the music of "Let's Go Fly a Kite" *from the soundtrack of* "Mary Poppins"

Let's go buy a gun
Where we'll all have fun
Let's go buy a gun and kill the bad guys
Hooray for the NRA
For that's the American way
Let's all go buy a gun

Let's kill birds of prey
Deer, boars all the day
Let's kill bears and foxes, elk and oxen
Children who play their games
Maiming, killing all the same
But let's all go buy a gun

Freedom and Liberty
Wave the flag and sing with me

God and country standing up and fighting together
We will not be slammed
Gun safety Hell be damned
Let's all go buy a gun

Military guns we need
To watch Bambi twist and bleed
Bigger guns we all do prize to compensate for our cock size
Jesus carried and told you this
To load and shoot's no greater bliss
So let's all go buy a gun

Smith, Wesson, Cabot, Colt
Winchester gives a bolt
Dillon, Daisy, Heckler and Koch for all us high velocity folk
Gun makers that's the way
With NRA to leaders pay
So let's all go buy a gun

Protecting my family
My castle, my right to be
More risk from those that we do know than strangers in home
    invasion
The U.S. tops the world
With guns and deaths and flags unfurled
But let's all go buy more guns

Countless innocents killed each year
But let us be completely clear
No restrictions to limit our rights will we let pass through
That is our battle cry
One which we live and die
Let's all go buy a gun

So gun control freaks leave us alone
Or we will come invade *your* homes
My rights you will never abridge 'cause we are stronger

We don't care how many die
Cause death's American as apple pie
So let's all go buy a gun
Yeah let's all go buy a gun
Now we've all gone to buy a gun (or ten).

Chapter Thirty-Seven

Santa Claus Shot and Killed in Home Invasion

Reported by Dr. Warren J. Blumenfeld

Breaking News: Santa Claus, of unknown age, was shot and killed by home owner, Jack Koff, 41, for allegedly breaking into and entering his residence at 007 Patriarchy Lane without authorization. The deceased was found wearing a bright red cap and full-body microfiber suit with white piping around the collar, sleeves, and pant legs. He also sported a full white beard and bushy eyebrows.

Tossed near the bullet-riddled body was a large canvas bag filled with brightly colored wrapped packages. Police department evidence officials later discovered that the boxes were filled with children's toys.

According to police Lieutenant Justin Tyme, "We have clear indication that Mr. Claus penetrated the home by shimmying down the chimney. We believe this because his clothing contained large amounts of ash and grime."

Responding to reporters' questions on the porch of his home, Koff stated that around 3:00 a.m. on the morning of December 25, while he and his wife and three lovely children were asleep on the second floor of their residence, he was startled out of a deep sleep by the apparent sounds of a pack of animals walking across the roof. Fearing a home invasion, Koff took his AK-47 rifle from his bedroom closet and walked slowly and silently down the stairs. As he reached the living room, he saw the image of an intruder exiting the fireplace.

"I took aim and fired a number of rounds into the guy," said Koff. "I have three young kids, and I'm not going to let some pansy pervert come into my home."

The town coroner, Helen A. Basket, determined that Claus died instantly with numerous bullet wounds to the head and upper back with one puncturing his heart. At a press conference held later in the day, Police Chief Reed Mylipps indicated that while the incident is still under investigation, at this point his department does not intend to press charges against Mr. Koff since it appears to be a case of justifiable homicide.

Claus leaves behind a wife, nine flying reindeer – one with a bright red nose – and a gaggle of elves. The coroner's office shipped the body back to his home at the North Pole where Ms. Claus will bury him on New Year's Day in a private ceremony.

This is the second incidence of the shooting deaths of home invaders on Patriarchy Lane in just the last three days. On Tuesday, homeowner Lance Boyle killed M&M Red and M&M Green as they filled bowls around his house with what appeared to be sweet chocolate centers – some which included peanuts – surrounded by hard candy shells. Boyle splattered Red and Green's little bodies on the walls and ceiling of his living and dining rooms leaving nothing for the coroner to autopsy.

Addressing the public during a nationally televised speech today, Wayne La Peter, spokesperson for the Nationalist Rifle Association, asserted: "The justifiable shootings of Claus, and M&M Red and Green prove our point when we rightfully argue that 'The only thing that blows away a bad dude with or without a gun is a good dude with a gun'!"

La Peter urged the relatively few home and apartment dwellers who have not already purchased *at least* one hand gun, one hunting rifle, and one semi-automatic firearm to run to the gun stores and buy them soon. He reminded parents that weapons not only save lives, but firearms also provide great ways to bond with their children.

"There's nothing greater than pulverizing paper and clay targets on the shooting range with your kids on the weekends," he said. "This is real quality time."

According to La Peter, "Keep up the great work America!"

Index

EQUITY IN HIGHER EDUCATION
THEORY, POLICY, & PRAXIS

A BOOK SERIES FOR EQUITY SCHOLARS & ACTIVISTS

Virginia Stead, H.B.A., B.Ed., M.Ed., Ed.D., *General Editor*

Globalization increasingly challenges higher education researchers, administrators, faculty members, and graduate students to address urgent and complex issues of equitable policy design and implementation. This book series provides an inclusive platform for discourse about—though not limited to—diversity, social justice, administrative accountability, faculty accreditation, student recruitment, admissions, curriculum, pedagogy, online teaching and learning, completion rates, program evaluation, cross-cultural relationship-building, and community leadership at all levels of society. Ten broad themes lay the foundation for this series but potential editors and authors are invited to develop proposals that will broaden and deepen its power to transform higher education:

(1) Theoretical books that examine higher education policy implementation,
(2) Activist books that explore equity, diversity, and indigenous initiatives,
(3) Community-focused books that explore partnerships in higher education,
(4) Technological books that examine online programs in higher education,
(5) Financial books that focus on the economic challenges of higher education,
(6) Comparative books that contrast national perspectives on a common theme,
(7) Sector-specific books that examine higher education in the professions,
(8) Educator books that explore higher education curriculum and pedagogy,
(9) Implementation books for front line higher education administrators, and
(10) Historical books that trace changes in higher education theory, policy, and praxis.

Expressions of interest for authored or edited books will be considered on a first come basis. A Book Proposal Guideline is available on request. For individual or group inquiries please contact:

Dr. Virginia Stead, General Editor | *virginia.stead@alum.utoronto.ca*

To order other books in this series, please contact our Customer Service Department at:

peterlang@presswarehouse.com (within the U.S.)
orders@peterlang.com (outside the U.S.)

Or browse online by series at www.peterlang.com

www.ingramcontent.com/pod-product-compliance
Lightning Source LLC
Chambersburg PA
CBHW071019280326
41935CB00011B/1410